LIVE *and* LET LOVE

LIVE *and* LET LOVE

NOTES FROM EXTRAORDINARY

WOMEN ON THE LAYERS,

THE LAUGHTER,

AND THE LITTER OF LOVE

Edited and with an Introduction by

Andrea Buchanan

GALLERY BOOKS

New York London Toronto Sydney

G

GALLERY BOOKS

A Division of Simon & Schuster, Inc.
1230 Avenue of the Americas
New York, NY 10020

Copyright © 2011 by Alligator Cowgirl Productions, Inc.

All rights reserved, including the right to reproduce this book or portions thereof in any form whatsoever. For information address Gallery Books Subsidiary Rights Department, 1230 Avenue of the Americas, New York, NY 10020

First Gallery Books hardcover edition February 2011

GALLERY BOOKS and colophon are trademarks of Simon & Schuster, Inc.

For information about special discounts for bulk purchases, please contact Simon & Schuster Special Sales at 1-866-506-1949 or business@simonandschuster.com.

The Simon & Schuster Speakers Bureau can bring authors to your live event. For more information or to book an event contact the Simon & Schuster Speakers Bureau at 1-866-248-3049 or visit our website at www.simonspeakers.com.

Manufactured in the United States of America

1   3   5   7   9   10   8   6   4   2

Library of Congress Cataloging-in-Publication Data

Live and let love : notes from extraordinary women on the layers, the laughter, and the litter of love / edited and with an introduction by Andrea Buchanan. — First Gallery Books harcover ed.
p.   cm.
1. Love—Religious aspects—Christianity.   2. Man-woman relationships.   3. Self-realization in women.   4. Spiritual life.   I. Buchanan, Andrea.
BV4639.L58   2011
306.7092'2—dc22   2010042668

ISBN 978-1-4391-9508-6

For my parents,
Buck and Sue, fifty-nine years and counting

CONTENTS

LIVE *and* LET LOVE

INTRODUCTION

*T*here is nothing more universal than love. It's what we desire to feel, adore to bestow, fight to achieve, and grieve when it's gone. Some would say love is the reason we are here . . . to give and receive it.

Since the dawn of humankind, love has been studied, pondered, pontificated and written about by scholars and sages of antiquity. From Aristotle to Austen to Ephron, love unadorned and unrequited has been in style. The Holy Bible is one of the oldest texts to talk about love and can likely be credited with starting the infinite fad: love is essential to living a faithful life. One passage I find particularly striking in its definition of love and its meaning was written by the Apostle Paul in I Corinthians:13.

> *And though I have the gift of prophecy, and understand all mysteries, and all knowledge; and though I have all faith, so that I can remove mountains, and have not love, I am nothing.*

I first started to understand that passage when I was fourteen years old. Saint Paul imparted to me that even with exalted powers, and surrounded by gifts, without love everything else is meaningless. I grew up in Texas and I had "found God" in a small, nondenominational Bible church. No one else in my family went to church but me. I was in search of meaning and had deep questions about faith, but I also had a crush on a boy, who would become my high school sweetheart. He was fifteen, had a car, and I was allowed to ride in it with him as long as I went to church and came straight home. So I did, religiously, to every Sunday service (morning and night) and Wednesday evenings for Bible Study. I would hold Ben's hand on our car rides, and during the Sunday youth group pizza parties. Early on in this phase, I memorized I Corinthians: 13, and would recite it to myself. I was falling in love for the first time and I felt that the words in Corinthians had been written just for *me.* It was a magical time and I can still recall the way I felt when I was around Ben like it was yesterday. It was so new, so innocent and pure. Whether we were driving with the windows down on a hot Texas summer night, or enjoying a first kiss under the bleachers after a Friday night football game, or discovering one another under the blankets on a van ride to Colorado, falling in love for the first time was a religious experience.

Six years and a couple of painful breakups later, Ben and I had moved on to different colleges and other relationships. God, as defined by the Church, became less important to me. Love, on the other hand, was still a supremely high priority. During this time, I embarked upon what would become a protracted journey through bridesmaid's hell, where love hides, usually under yards upon yards of taffeta. Participating in the first wedding where I had to buy my own dress and matching shoes, I took my place next to the other eight best friends and bridesmaids, and I had an unexpected pang of beautiful memories and love lost when the preacher read from Corinthians. He also took the opportunity to invite anyone who had not been saved in his captive audience to come up and accept Jesus Christ as their saviour before the groom kissed the bride. I like a good "two for one" sale, but even I thought it was a bit cheap. About that time, I saw my father, who is a striking six foot one and easily agitated, stand up and walk out of the church to go have a smoke, while my beautiful mother stayed patiently in her seat. He was an agnostic, bordering on atheist, and unsavable, and she would never leave before the curtain call. After a few lost souls found their salvation as I did some knee bends to keep from fainting, the groom kissed the bride, the preacher read the famous verse, and I quietly wept, mourning the passing of my youthful first love, and wishing that one day I might have a wedding, without taffeta, but certainly with Corinthians.

> *Love is patient, love is kind. It does not envy, it does not boast, it is not proud. It is not rude, it is not self-seeking, it is not easily angered, it keeps no record of wrongs. Love does not delight in evil but rejoices with the truth. It always protects, always trusts, always hopes, always perseveres. Love never fails.*

While I no longer consider myself a practicing Christian, I consider biblical teachings along with philosophical texts from antiquity's timeless studies of love as more of an open-ended question than an absolute fact, and I highly value them as I attempt to understand love's layers and complexities. With love there is no absolute. There are some very smart people out there who have studied this topic extensively. I'm certainly not a scholar of love, with minimal courses in philosophy at the University of North Texas under my belt. My understanding of love comes from the school of hard knocks. I speak from my own experiences of my heart opening and shattering from love fulfilled and unrequited, as do my fellow storytellers in this book.

However, for a moment I'll put my scholarly shortcomings aside to offer a quick refresher. The English etymology of the word "love" derives from the Germanic form of the Sanskrit *lubh*—which means desire. And while desire certainly has something to do with feelings that seem like love, desire alone is not love. As we all know, there are so many more forms of love than just all-out-crazy-for-you lust. But lust can be a lot of fun—and sometimes dangerous, which can just add to the rush. Case in point: my college crush, who I'll call John. We were both sophomores when we met. He was a Sigma Phi Epsilon fraternity brother and I was an honorary little sister to the fraternity. He and I loved to dance, and somehow our grooves fit. Every time a song from the band New Order would come on at a party, we would find one another and clear the floor. Our connection was rhythmically deep, and I was madly in lust. John was a dangerous bad boy with a lot of hard edges, and an incredibly soft spirit. He was Patrick Swayze in *Dirty Dancing*, and I wanted to be his "Baby." He rode a motorcycle, every other word out of his mouth was of the four-letter variety, and when we weren't getting our groove on at fraternity parties we would travel the forty miles into downtown Dallas and dance until the clubs closed.

There was always an element of danger when I was with John, and yet I always felt safe, because he had that Alpha male, badass thing going on. There was an abandoned warehouse in downtown Dallas that he knew about that graffiti artists used as a canvas. We would break into it and leave our artistic imprint with a spray can, smoke some weed, and make out. It was in an undesirable and somewhat dangerous part of the city, and a far cry from my church days, but I loved the thrill of it. We were never officially boyfriend and girlfriend, but that was okay, I knew what we had was special, even if jail time was a possible consequence. I was hot for him and his Alpha nature. Philosophy invokes this kind of love as *Eros*—the part of love constituting sexual desire and passion. Erotic love is fun, it's sometimes dangerous, and I believe it's necessary, for without it none of us would exist. I'm pretty sure John would agree.

The passionate relationship that John and I shared, over time turned into more of a fondness and friendship. Aristotle was obsessed with this kind of love, which he called *Philia*—a fondness of one's family, friends, political community, job, or discipline. Loving family and friends comes pretty easily to most people. Loving a job is a different story. I realize that in today's world, where so many people are unemployed, the idea that you love what you do is often a foreign concept. In a perfect world, we would all love our work, but life certainly isn't perfect and loving what you do is a luxury that not everyone can afford. I've been fortunate in the work department and found something I love to do, but it wasn't always the case.

As a longtime producer of television in Hollywood, I had begun to feel dissatisfied with the kinds of projects I was involved with. So in 2004, an election year, I decided to make a documentary film with some friends about the March for Women's Lives in Washington, D.C. While the gig didn't pay well, it was thrilling to be at the helm of a project that I found meaningful. My political activist side was lit up and I knew that for me, finding meaning in my work life was no longer a luxury, it was an absolute necessity. After that project ended and I found myself in a black hole of filming reality television shows, I longed for something more. I longed to be in love with my work. Like some of the contributors who share their stories in the pages to come, I think falling in love with what you do can absolutely result in a healthy, satisfying relationship that offers plenty of sustainment, in addition to the belief that finding love in another person will come.

The final kind of love as defined by the Greek philosophers is beyond the earthly pleasures of lust, family, and work. It is the all-encompassing *Agape*, which, appropriated by Christian theology, is the paternal love of God for man and man for God. However, I would argue that *Agape* is the purest form of love for each other. The concept that love is peace and mutual respect, if truly practiced and adopted, might end all war. Imagine that! John Lennon certainly did, and along with the other fab three put that idea into words, giving us some of the best love songs ever written. "All you need is Love"—the Beatles abridged Corinthians!

A primer on how great thinkers define love wouldn't be complete if I didn't include the man who wrote arguably the most powerful works on the subject: the Bard himself. Anyone who has ever fallen hard can identify with Shakespeare's plays— particularly if they pick up one of his tragedies in the aftermath of getting dumped, since Shakespeare's idea of love unfulfilled was tragic. You either *love* or *you die*, in the case of Romeo and Juliet or Hamlet and Ophelia.

When Ben, my first love, let go of my hand and broke up with me, I felt like Juliet and Ophelia one hundred times over. I stopped eating. I cried all day, every day. I cried before school; during math, history, and English classes; and after school working as a checkout girl at the Tom Thumb grocery store. The bags under my eyes were so big I could have packed them and gone on vacation. I literally begged Ben to take me back, in between sobs, sitting in his banana yellow Cutlass Supreme, where our hand-holding began. I told him I couldn't live without him, and I meant it. He was very sweet when he told me he was sorry, it was over. And to top it off, my tragedy played out the same week of cheerleading tryouts, which in Texas is tantamount to the Olympic Trials with pom-poms. To add salt to the already open wound, I didn't make the cheerleading team. It was Rejection with a capital R. Fortunately, no one in my Shakespearean tragedy died. But it felt like death at the time.

Eventually, I replaced the Shakespearean tragedy with a Hollywood movie, "love at first sight" moment that I sometimes, even to this day, find hard to believe. Sixteen years ago I met my husband, Jason, in a smoky, dimly lit bar thanks to an introduction by Paul Rudd, who was just starting his acting career. Jason had just returned from a summer at Oxford University where he studied classical theater with the Juilliard School, and Jason and Paul became close friends. Paul convinced Jason to make the move from New York to Los Angeles to pursue acting and he had been in Los Angeles exactly two weeks the night I met him. Jason was a brooding artist, handsome, and he was fluent in French. I thought he was out of my league, not just because of the sexy foreign language thing, not to mention the Oxford thing, but because I didn't believe at the time that I might actually fall in love with someone who would not only love me back but catch me when I fell and give me a hand so that I could get up.

Up until meeting Jason, I kept trying to engage in love to please the other person. After a particularly one-sided romance with a much older man who gave me a jar of Dijon mustard for my twenty-third birthday, and the period of celibacy and self-searching that ensued, by my twenty-fifth birthday I was ready to be in a relationship again. My dear friend and roommate, Jill, and I did an improvised "rain dance" in our kitchen, only we wanted it to rain boyfriends for each of us. We were very specific with our wishes: the guys had to be romantic, generous, enlightened, mature, smart, respectful, and nice. Which, at the time, seemed like a tall order, considering that my last boyfriend, the Dijon-giver, broke up with me on Valentine's Day. Within a week after that dance, I walked into that smoky bar with a sense of peace and joy, and the proverbial lightning strike happened the moment I met Jason. I remember saying to Jill, "I'm going to marry that guy," like it was yesterday. The words flew out of my mouth as easy as "I'll have another drink." I didn't intellectualize the thought, I just felt it, and then I declared it. It was a feeling that was born out of a primal instinct, a knowledge that the potential for love was in the room and with my potential life partner.

Jason and I didn't rush into a wedding, by any stretch. It took us about eight years, and a lot of back-and-forth, to finally make that commitment. By that point, all my years as a bridesmaid, standing in taffeta, dreaming of the day where I would hear Corinthians, felt like someone else's life rather than my own. That girl was long gone, and this new L.A. woman, who had looked for love in all the wrong places, was independent, somewhat confident, and certainly didn't feel like she needed a marriage license to be loved. The truth was, I was terrified to commit on that level, on a government level, on a level that if I ever wanted to get out, I would need a lawyer, not just some cash in the bank and my car.

But the big day arrived, and I have a picture from it that I adore. The image is of my father walking behind me holding my gorgeous Vera Wang gown that my sister, Cindy, so generously bought for me, so that it wouldn't drag in the dirt. It was an out-door wedding, at a friend's estate in the Hollywood Hills, and the aisle consisted of a dirt path surrounded by ominous, large, prehistoric cacti. In the photograph it looks as though I am running and my dad is pushing me down the makeshift aisle, because if I take my time, I might change my mind. My mouth is making an O shape, and the caption, if there was one, would read: "Oh shit, I can't believe I'm doing this." It's definitely not your typical serene, hopeful, smiling bride photo-op, but more along the lines of Calamity Jane meets Runaway Bride.

As we stood in the middle of a big circle of our friends with a Sikh guru and beloved friend as our officiant and minister, we included Jewish prayers, Native American rituals, and the Beatles' "In My Life" played on an aluminum cello bellowing across the canyon. I framed that picture of me and my dad, and it sits on my nightstand to remind me of how far I've come; that my fear of losing my freedom or my identity was ultimately just a feeling, and that I would have never married Jason if losing either one was going to be part of the deal. The truth is I feel more liberated in this partnership than I did out of it. It was a beautiful day, and while we didn't read from Corinthians, it was absolutely divine.

Four years after our wedding day, I codirected and wrote a short film about love and longevity in a marriage. In the script, Kris Kristofferson, who plays the husband, is caring for his dying wife in an E.R. When asked by a young nurse played by Robin Wright what the secret to love was, he says, "Stay in the room," which accounts for the theme of the film and speaks to the idea of not leaving when things get really difficult and when things don't come easy. That life lesson was imparted to me from a beloved therapist to many of my friends, and in turn to me through them, and we have used it throughout the years whether we are talking about our friendships or our romantic relationships. By staying in the room there won't always be lightning strikes, although those still happen, but more like small fires that continue to burn if they are stoked.

My life with Jason is the warm glowing fire that can peak with vibrant flames—and we have stayed in the room together when the oxygen was thin and breathing was difficult. We've managed to emerge stronger through it all, build a home, rescue and raise dogs, go through midlife crises, travel the world, and laugh until our cheeks hurt. And it's in this relationship and the laughter and the litter that I have learned more about love than anything else in my life. And the most profound self-love lesson that I have learned is that *I am enough.*

When I set out to collect stories about love, I was narrowly focused on the Eros brand of love stories; the romance, the passion, the humor, and the redemptions. Not the Shakespear-ean kind per se, more the *Sex and the City* kind. However, along the way the collection became so much richer and deeper, thanks to the contributors' willingness and courage to look the topic in the face and then look within themselves to find their strongest examples of it. Each woman in this book has her own love story that is up close and personal. The essays are reflec-tions of joy and suffering from love, and within those layers, there are gems of wisdom and precious self-realizations that need to be shared. They are pictures of vulnerability, wickedly funny, and one hundred percent raw, and they have added to the long narrative of love. In short, the women in this book are truly awe-inspiring. I love each and every one of them.

My journey has taken me from the Bible to the Beatles, Eros to happily ever after, and while I still have a lot to learn on the topic of love, I do know this: It is messy, it is heartbreaking, and God, is it worth it. It is my wish that if you allow the layers, the laughter, and the litter of love to envelop you, then you will not only have loved but you will have truly and fully *lived*.

APB
September 13, 2010

The Most Unselfish Love

MARIA BELLO

Maria Bello is an award-winning actress with many diverse roles in films such as *The Cooler* and *A History of Violence*, along with close to thirty others. She began her career as an activist at Villanova University, where she majored in Peace and Justice Education, and since then her activist work has taken her around the globe from Darfur to Honduras to Haiti. For the last three years she has worked in Haiti with Artists for Peace and Justice, raising funds and awareness of the extreme poverty there and the plight of women and children. Six days after the January 2010 earthquake she brought emergency relief supplies to Port-au-Prince and continues her work there both politically and as a humanitarian. A proud mother to her son, Bello lives in Los Angeles.

On December 5, 2008, I was witness to the most unselfish act of love I could have ever imagined. More than a year before the devastating earthquake in January 2010 that claimed more than 250,000 lives in Haiti, I went to visit the impoverished but beautiful country and my life would never be the same.

I had traveled with a group of friends to the opening of Kay Germaine, the first hospital for disabled children in Port-au-Prince, Haiti. My friend Paul Haggis had met Father Rick Frechette, a priest and doctor who had been working with the poorest of the poor in Haiti for twenty-three years and invited a group of us to witness his work. The first thing you notice about Father are his striking blue eyes and his ever-present smile. He looks like Paul Newman but with a hearty laugh and wicked sense of humor. Father had been a priest working in Haiti for twenty-two years; an American boy from Connecticut, he had gone to Haiti to work with the poorest of the poor in the slums, and when he realized they needed a doctor as much as a priest, he started traveling back to the States each week to take classes and get his medical degree.

Over his years of service, he has built three orphanages and thirty-two schools in the Cite Soleil slums. He delivers the only free drinking water there, feeds 3,500 people a week and gives free medical care to children. He built St. Damien's pediatric hospital, a bakery, a mechanic shop, sewing facilities, and now Kay Germaine for disabled kids. Give Father a dollar and he will turn it into a hundred in a day to help those in need.

Though I was present as much as I could be, I was not in a very good place in my life. I was traveling with my then boyfriend, and our relationship was falling apart. We would visit the hospital and then come back to our little room and fight like crazy. My eight-year-old was at home in LA, and I was beating myself up for leaving him for three days. I hadn't worked for months and was worried about how I would pay my son's tuition in the spring. I was perhaps experiencing a bout of depression, which I have struggled with my whole life. I was beating myself up constantly over all of the things I *should* be doing and feeling worthless that I could not do them all. I felt lost at sea and couldn't seem to find my footing and somehow couldn't remember who I was. I was overwhelmed and exhausted and on the first night ended up crying myself to sleep.

For three days, we followed Father through his community. During the first two days we spent with him we stood by him as he expertly diagnosed a malnourished child, held the mother of a dying boy, delivered huge bags of rice, visited his schools in the slums, lead the most joyous service for the disabled children at the new hospital, and drank red wine with us at midnight. The man, it seemed, never slept. And on the evening that he took us in an open-air truck to what is called the "most dangerous slum in the world," men, women, and children ran after us, laughing and yelling in Creole, "our Father, our Father!" And he laughed and extended his hand and introduced us to the children who attended his schools, living in streets littered with mountains of trash and eating "mud cakes" made of mud and flour.

We spent our afternoons in St. Damien's hospital, holding children and changing diapers and giving a hand when one was needed to the tireless and committed staff. On the second afternoon, there was a baby who caught my eye I was particularly drawn to. She looked like she was about six weeks old and had tubes in her nose and arms. Her name, I saw on her chart, was Fedaline. She was one of many abandoned children in Port-au-Prince and was left at the hospital perhaps because her limbs were atrophied and her parents could not take care of her. Of all the many sick children there, for some reason I was most drawn to her. She lay in her bassinette whimpering, too exhausted or sick to really cry. She looked up at me with wet, brown eyes, and I reached down and saw that she was sopping wet. Like any mom would have, I picked her up and changed her diaper. I held her for a bit til she stopped crying and laid her back down.

In the midst of such tragedy, I couldn't help thinking about my own small life. I thought, "Look at these people who work tirelessly every day to help these kids. What the hell am I doing with my life? Fighting with my boyfriend? Making movies?" Needless to say, I felt like a bit of a dope. My contribution to this world, whatever it was, suddenly didn't seem to matter in the least. Leaving Fedaline, my heart was heavy with self-judgment.

Being witness to all this helped me for a moment not to fight with my boyfriend or obsess about my child, but nothing could have prepared us for what we witnessed on the third day. We had heard rumblings of Father "burying the dead," and that day we were to discover why people spoke of this with such gratitude and respect in their voices. Children died in the hospital every day, and the overwhelmed city morgue received two hundred or so bodies a week, so Father and his crew would pick up the bodies and bury them in the papier-mâché coffins that he taught his staff to make. He does this most unselfish act every day to give these poor men, women, and children with no names some dignity in their deaths, which most of them probably never had in their lives.

On that sunny morning, ten of us accompanied Father to the front of the hospital as he blessed the hundred or so women who lined up every day, holding sick children in their arms, hoping to be admitted. (Only the sickest ones would be.) Then, silently, we followed him to a tiny room on the third floor of the hospital. Seeing him dressed in his priest robes for the first time since we'd met him, and standing in the prayerful silence of his crew, we knew something holy was about to take place.

There were two small tables in the room. On each one laid a package in white butcher paper. As Father started to speak, we realized what was in those packages. It was the children who had died the night before. Father spoke of the innocence of these angels, how, no matter if they were abandoned, name-less, and faceless, they were all God's gifts and had touched this world in some way. He talked of Mary Magdalene, who washed the feet of Jesus, and what a selfless act that was, a sign of re-spect for all people. A woman stepped forward and unwrapped the first package and started to wash the emaciated frame of a twelve-year-old boy as Father told us how, when Mary Magda-lene washed the feet of Jesus, it was a blessing to him and to herself.

Father joined her and gently washed the child with a warm sponge; he held him in his arms and prayed for him and wrapped him in linen cloths, which a group of women from a church in the Midwest had embroidered with crosses and hearts. We watched silently and in awe as he gently placed one of the children back down and opened the next package. The tiny baby inside was Fedaline.

Father looked at me with a kind smile. It was as if he knew what my connection was to her and that I was supposed to step forward. Part of me thought, "Man up and do what needs to be done." The other part, the lost part, thought, "No fucking way, I'm no saint. If I had to do a confession with Father right now it would take thirty days and nights." And yet when I looked at Father, I felt somehow that it was my duty to wash her, as if the synchronicity was too great to ignore and something was forcing me to walk toward her. And I did.

I took the sponge and began to do what I had seen Father do. As I bathed her arms, which were soft and limp, I forgot about my boyfriend and how unworthy I was and how I wasn't enough and how little my life meant. I suddenly felt that she had blessed me by choosing me to hold her in her last hours of life, and I was now a proud witness to her passing. And something shifted in me at that moment. I think my heart became a little more malleable, a little softer, a little more forgiving of myself and others. I truly felt that she was now an angel, blessing me with the words, "It's okay. You are loved. And you ain't half bad." Words I needed to hear.

After the ceremony, Father took off his robes, gave us a smile, and said, "What a beautiful day!" before climbing onto the roof to fix an antenna.

All of us who witnessed Father's grace that day will never be the same. I know that somehow he sensed my pain and believed that in the gift of service I could be healed. He understood the gift of grace that caring for a dead child could bring. He did this every day. Could there be a more selfless act of love than to bury an abandoned child? There is no one to say thank you, no parents weeping and taking the child away, no pats on the back. I got a taste of his life, his deep humility in the face of grace.

Now, two years later, having spent much more time with Father Rick, I know he would be mortified to read this! He would say that I made him sound like a saint, which he is not. He would say he is just doing what needs to be done. That it is the poor in Haiti, living in the most horrific conditions but making a decision every day to believe in beauty and hope and love in the midst of their poverty, who are the real heroes. He would say that grace isn't a gift only given to priests and saints but to nameless children and actresses who have forgotten who they are.

Note to self:

**There is grace
in pure love.**

Since the earthquake in January, Father Rick has started a hospital for the deaf and blind, an adult hospital, the first free secondary school in Port-au-Prince, a women's health and maternity center, and . . . the list goes on.

To find more about Father Rick and his work go to APJNOW.org.

The Chicken or the Egg

ORITTE BENDORY

Oritte Bendory is a New York–based writer, blogger, and producer. Bendory grew up in New Jersey and lived in Los Angeles for six years, where she produced independent films and wrote screenplays, including one purchased by Twentieth Century Fox. She moved back to New York several years ago and is working on her first novel, a sensitive portrait of a marriage in crisis set in Hollywood. Bendory also writes a blog about dating and divorce, and all the Jewish guilt that goes with it, called "The Cougel Chronicles: Tales of a Jewish Cougar."

When I left my husband after fourteen years of dating and marriage, I wasn't thinking about time, or the age I'd be when I eventually emerged from the wreckage. I was thirty-five, and all I could think about was saving myself. I felt like I was drowning, being sucked down by a churning vortex, and I had to get out of the water, fast. My singular goal was clawing my way to dry land at all costs, nothing more. It didn't matter that my husband was trying to get me to stay by highlighting what he knew to be my biggest fears. If I left him, I'd be out there alone,

THE CHICKEN OR THE EGG

for the first time in my life. If I left him, I could kiss my dream of living a certain kind of life goodbye. But mostly, if I left him, I could lose my chance at having a child. He referenced my age, reminding me that my ovaries were not as young as they used to be. I was no spring chicken.

I hadn't paused to consider it. A drowning man does not think about his hopes and dreams, about the one thing he wants and will regret not having most, when he is fighting for his life. So, when making my choice between staying married and having a baby, or saving myself and figuring it out later, the choice seemed simple.

My husband and I were living in Los Angeles at the time. We had moved there from New York in our mid-twenties to pursue the far-fetched dream one can only attempt at a young and hopeful age: to make it in the movie business. We wrote together and our scripts were our babies. There was no room in our lives for a real live breathing one, nor were we willing to trade in anything to make the space for it. We both came from large, close-knit families, and we took it for granted that having kids of our own was something we would eventually get around to. We were immune to feeling the passage of time, perpetuated by the lack of seasons in California. It didn't help that all the while we were surrounded by people with the same attitude as us: actors, writers, and directors who put their fledgling careers before all else, and behaved as if they would be young forever, hanging out in cafés, surfing, and partying like kids. We felt like kids, too, so how could we consider having any?

When we separated, the protective bubble burst. Suddenly, the adolescent lifestyle we had perpetuated, and the six years we had lost pursuing an elusive dream, reared its ugly head.

The choices we had made and the price that had been paid for them was flagrant. But I was unable to confront the repercussions yet; the only life I knew had evaporated into thin air. I was leaving my husband, my best friend and partner since college, as well as Hollywood and our shared life and aspirations. I had no reason to stay in Los Angeles, and decided to move back to New York to be near my parents and sisters, where I wouldn't be alone. And yet, I felt more alone than ever.

I soon discovered that this disorienting journey, by the sheer emotional travel time, creates an acute and never-ending feeling of jetlag. The kind you want to just sleep off. I kept anxiously pressing the fast-forward button on my life, but it failed me every time. I wanted to sleep away the pain and yearned for time to magically leap forward, so I could wake up one year later, with the dislocation—and the grief—banished.

But apparently that's not how life works. There are no detours around grief, no shortcuts to healing. This time, I would have to inhabit every molecule of time and endure its passage. I could no longer ignore it as I had when I was married and living in La-La land. But still, my biological clock ticking did not factor into the equation. This new stage of my life was strictly about surviving the grief and depression; it was about "getting through it."

Two years later, when the fog cleared and my drawn-out and litigious divorce was finally official, my husband's words sank in like long, sharp teeth. There I was, single at thirty-seven, and I was definitely no spring chicken. I had secured a job in a small advertising firm, where my coworkers anticipated my occasional emotional outbursts and were careful not to push my divorce buttons. But then a new hire, a twenty-four-year-old hipster, oblivious to what I had been through, alarmingly called me "Cougs" (short for Cougar). I told myself that he intended it as a compliment to my appearance, rather than as a disparagement of my age.

I knew I looked young. People often thought I was twenty-nine. It was as if my arrested development had frozen both my physical and emotional maturation in time; if only it had done the same thing to my eggs. I knew I wasn't wrinkled or out of shape yet, nor was I afraid of that happening. I was afraid of my fertility dropping off and disappearing. On some nights I could hear my eggs plotting and whispering in tiny cartoon voices, packing up their bags in preparation to hightail it out of there. I tried to coerce them to stay just a little while longer by using all sorts of rationalizations provided by my girlfriends, who insisted that "we" had plenty of time. But my girlfriends were thirty-two, with eggs five years younger than mine. It wasn't the same. Even my own well-intentioned mother bombarded me with evidence—research and statistics from fertility specialists she must have Googled—which proved women today could get pregnant until forty-five, including her friend's daughter, whom she ran into at a Shiva call. Amidst a houseful of mourners grieving their beloved, my mother managed to phone me and whisper that this woman, who was forty-one, recently had twins.

"Good for her," I said, not meaning it. Unlike me, my mother's friend's daughter had planned such critical steps in advance, and in the right order, too. She had her twins with her husband of eight years, using eggs she froze in her early thirties and fertilized later with his sperm. But it was different for me. I no longer had a sperm-ready husband, nor did I see any prospects on the horizon. Whenever I saw my parents and my sisters, they pressured me to get out there and find someone. On a rainy night, on a visit to see them in New Jersey for my niece's birthday, my father picked me up from the train station, but when I got into his car, he didn't pull it out of the parking spot. Instead, he turned to me and said, "A woman like you, at your age, needs to be a husband hunter." Up until that moment, I believed that I was making progress; that I could handle this kind of advice. But my outburst conveyed the opposite. Tears sprung into my eyes and I pumped my fist on the dashboard and yelled: "I don't want another f——g husband!"

It dawned on me that, no, I didn't want another husband. Surely not then; maybe not ever. I had already had one in my lifetime, and maybe that was enough. I wanted more time to figure it out. I felt that after everything I'd been through, hell, I deserved more time.

Tough shit, mocked my fleeing eggs. Or was it the echo of my husband's voice taunting me? I couldn't tell the difference. The point was, whether or not I felt emotionally ready to find a partner was irrelevant; my fertility couldn't care less. And then it hit me: I was in the midst of another divorce. Not with another person, but with my biological clock; something that was part of me, that I could not control, negotiate with, or rid myself of. I was stuck. I could not bear to envision my future without a biological child, and yet I felt bereft of the tools and readiness necessary to have one.

Then I found Jeff. Although he had already found me. Jeff had been right under my nose for a year and a half, a devoted friend who dropped whatever he was doing when I needed him. When I sprained my ankle on a bad date, stepping off the curb in heels

I hated, I forced myself to walk normally for four blocks, until the guy and I parted ways. I collapsed inside my apartment, unable to make it further than the front door, and called Jeff. It was one o'clock in the morning, and my phone call woke him. Twenty minutes later, after taking a cab from Queens, he came to my rescue. He carried me to the couch and wrapped my ankle in a bag of frozen peas that he'd grabbed from his apartment at the last minute. I hated peas growing up, but I loved them then.

Jeff was from a small town in the South where nice people are made, aptly named "Niceville." He was the kind of guy every sensible young woman wishes for. He loved me unwaveringly, and eventually I realized I loved him too. But there was one problem: Jeff was twenty-six, almost eleven years my junior. He had a meager salary, a roommate who he liked to order pizza with, and—worst of all—he glowed with the irritating exuberance of unjaded youth. There was something about that untainted excitement, that unblemished soul, that pissed me off. It was as if his lack of baggage was an affront to my own; in a way it made mine feel heavier. I wished he was five years farther along, or that I was five years younger, closer to his stage in life. If only I had woken up and left my husband just a few years sooner, it might have been possible for me to join Jeff at the same point on life's ladder and have a relationship with him. For a brief, fleeting period, I managed to trick myself into believing that this was possible. Jeff and I dated for several heady summer months, where I allowed myself to be free, young, and in love in New York City, a feeling I had never before experienced. I paused time once again, and muted the ticking of the clock.

It was tempting to live that way forever; or at least for a year or two. But soon enough the gap in our age and experience threatened to swallow us up again, and although I wasn't necessarily ready to have a baby just then, I knew for certain that I wanted one soon. And Jeff didn't know what he wanted yet. How could he?

When we broke up, I found myself sifting through the pain of a failed relationship once again. But more so, I was grieving the loss of what I believed was my last chance to have a baby with a partner (while also proving my husband wrong). I realized that I had been holding tightly to that fantasy, hoping that if Jeff and I could make it work, I would be able to have a biological child with him before that window of opportunity slammed shut for good. I found it unusually cruel that right when I was finally able to take a hard look at my life and my future, the universe threw a great guy in my path, but with the biggest obstacle between us being the thing that plagued me most: age and time.

Like most things that become clear only in retrospect, I eventually realized that my relationship with Jeff was not one of life's acts of malice at all; it was a gift. By coming into my life, Jeff had exposed my issue with time and age and pushed me out of stasis—propelling me forward—while also giving me a taste of hope and love. Our breakup was actually a reconciliation in disguise, forcing me to finally come to terms with my biological clock and accept the cards that had been dealt to me. The decision to let go of my marriage and the conventional path I had been on had come with a price; it turned me down a different and unfamiliar path, and I had to accept it, no matter how unconventional and frightening it appeared.

When I left Los Angeles almost three years ago, I sat next to an older woman on the lonely flight back to New York. At the time, I was drawn to her because she was unwed, and seemed wise and strong, while I felt vulnerable and weak. We spoke for a good portion of the trip. The part of her story that I had been unable to connect with back then occurred to me now: she had her eggs frozen at thirty-five, and when she turned forty, having not yet found a man to co-parent with her, she began the arduous process of searching for and securing a sperm donor. She was flying home, after a brief business trip in Los Angeles, to see her biological daughter who was about to turn three.

A few months after Jeff and I broke up, I remembered an email that my mother sent me after my divorce as part of her "you can still get pregnant" campaign. It contained the name of a specialist at NYU's Fertility Center, suggesting I set up a consultation. I'm pretty sure I ignored it; I might have even deleted it. But now I realized, what was the big deal? It was just a phone call, followed by an appointment to discuss my options. Because I still have options, even though they might be different than the ones I had previously envisioned for myself.

I set up the appointment. And after only one initial consultation, I was given the assurance—and the hope—that although I may no longer be a spring chicken, I still have plenty of eggs.

Note to self:

**Clocks should not
dictate what we do
with our time.**

Oceans Apart

ANASTASIA BROWN

Anastasia Brown is an award-winning, Nashville-based power player in the music industry. As a judge on USA Networks' Nashville Star, she was inspired to write a book offering guidance for aspiring artists, writers, and musicians, (*Make Me a Star*). A passionate activist and proud mother, Anastasia is committed to creating music and opportunities for artists, advocating causes, and developing filmed entertainment for years to come.

Falling in love is like dancing in the meadows. Falling in love with a friend and man I respected for years was like dancing in the heavens. I literally felt like I was floating at times and felt butterflies the size of Texas during our first kiss at the Pub of Love in Nashville. We had the same group of friends and both worked in the music industry. Before that first kiss, as a manager I pitched him artists like Keith Urban and John Berry to consider signing to his record label, and he in turn set up meetings with artists like Allison Moorer and Todd Snider for management consideration. After that first kiss, once the butterflies subsided, my first thought was, *Oh shit, have I ruined a great friendship and my career?*

Years earlier, when I was still in my twenties, I had mistaken infatuation for love, and began to have doubts about the mysterious notion of unconditional love. Although I witnessed it all my life watching my parents, I was under the impression that only a chosen few received that gift, not realizing that it's as much of a choice as it is bestowed. Then I gave birth to my beautiful son, Wilson, and thought to myself, *Wow, this is what love feels like!* Experiencing this cleared up all confusion, allowing me to recognize it five years later, and I quickly stopped worrying about the consequences to our friendship and my career brought on by that magical kiss.

After falling deeper in love with my friend, he flew to my parents' home in Florida to ask for my hand in marriage. My dad, or, as he's known, Father Dave (he's an Episcopal priest), and my mother, Katrina, grilled him, and he passed their test. I didn't know about the imminent proposal, so when my mom started asking me serious questions right before Christmas, I was understandably confused. At one point, she looked at me intently and asked, "How much do you love him?" I responded, "The way you love dad." Then she pried some more, and hauntingly inquired, "Do you love him enough to push him around in a wheelchair?" That question stopped me in my tracks. I actually paused and really considered my answer. "Yes, my love is that strong. I know I could do that if I had to."

Looking back at that moment, I remember having a sinking feeling that I may have to live up to that answer. But that nagging feeling was soon pushed aside by a romantic Christmas proposal, engagement, and my excitement for the upcoming fairy-tale wedding. During our engagement we went to marriage counseling (I really think it should become a requirement in order to receive a marriage license), and in those sessions we studied each and every vow, what they meant, and how we would be able to stay true to them during times of crisis. We "passed" marriage counseling and committed to the vows with a capital C. As I watched my new husband bond with my son Wilson, who was almost six at the time, it strengthened our union. Our love affair made us extremely preoccupied, and we got lost in each other's eyes at parties, dinners, on planes— every day of the week, several times a day. Our friends use to pretend to gag at times when they'd see how the world would melt away around us and all that was visible to one another was the two of us. It was so profound. I wouldn't have turned away from our commitment even if I knew what enormous pain our love would cause me in the future. I concur with Alfred, Lord Tennyson, "'Tis better to have loved and lost/Than never to have loved at all."

Three years after our fairy-tale wedding, the vow "in sickness and in health" became my reality when my husband, soul mate, and best friend suffered a traumatic brain injury. It's not my place to share his story, but I will share mine. As I flew to L.A. not knowing if he would be alive when I landed, all I could do was pray, but I didn't know which words to use. As we both have living wills, I knew what he wanted, so all I could say was, "Let Your will be done." Yet after racing through the hospital halls to find him being rolled into the first surgery, I saw him dying in front of my eyes. I knew at that moment without a doubt I was willing and able to stay true to that vow.

I prayed like I've never prayed before: "God, I'll push him in a wheelchair 'til the end of time, just please save him, save us. I don't want to live without him." I realized during that crisis I was strong enough to love unconditionally for a lifetime. What a gift it is to have that knowledge. As they always had, family and friends surrounded us with love and support; my soul sister left her music video set to be at my side; a girlfriend in Nashville sent panties to my hotel room; a friend in L.A. gave me her car to use while I set up a temporary home at a hotel across the street from UCLA; my best friend flew Wilson to L.A. after I spent weeks missing him; and my parents and sister held my hand trying to give me hope. The love I felt kept me going.

After a week of touch and go, two goodbyes in the ICU, fainting, panic attacks, pacing, and making more promises to God, the surgeon took me aside in the hospital hallway and used the "r" word for the first time: recovery. I hugged him and cried with joy, but his response to my excitement ran a chill down my spine. "I want to warn you that it's impossible to predict the long-term implications of any brain injury," he said, then closed with a comment that turned my stomach. "In fact, he may not love you or feel the same way about you after he recovers." Though momentarily sickened at the possibility, I thought, *We were given the miracle of life and we have true love—that won't happen to us!*

Then the waiting game began. Caring for someone you love who is in a coma for five weeks is indescribable. Almost in denial, I gave my husband massages, my father anointed him twice a day, and I obsessed over his intercranial pressure (or ICPs). One day I decided that music was the answer to lower his ICPs, in came the boombox, and my gig as his personal D.J. began. It was remarkable: when I played James Taylor, Norah Jones, or mellow classical music, his ICPs went down; if I played an artist he loves, like Lucinda Williams, his numbers would soar up, so I'd quickly rip the CD out of the player.

Then the "mini-miracles" began. Easter weekend, my "ICU angel," an amazing nurse who took care of my husband in the intensive-care unit for many weeks, invited me to a Good Friday service on the beach (only in L.A.). Water has always been cathartic for me, and experiencing this service so close to the ocean was such a gift. At the close of the rite we were invited to nail our burdens to a cross. Oh my, did I have some burdens to give to God, and I nailed them hard to the cross! As we were in that surreal setting, wiping tears away yet feeling God's love, we got a phone call: "He woke up." We raced back to the hospital to see him, but he was already back asleep. Yet days following that, when he heard us laugh, his eyes would pop open at that familiar sound, and it would be cause for a celebration. When we saw a toe move, a tiny smile, or when I felt him squeeze my hand, I experienced a similar emotion as I did when I felt my son move in my stomach for the first time.

The biggest challenge during times of crisis is to focus on the positive and push worst-case scenarios out of our thought patterns, but this is critical for the survival of both the patient and the caregiver. The first year of serving as nurse, driver, and medicine dispenser was fulfilling, yet I wonder if it tipped the balance between my husband and me as lovers. Can a man allow the inevitable vulnerability of dependency without harboring resentments? I still don't know.

Over the next six years, we went back to work creating music, and our life seemed to be back to normal on the outside; but it wasn't even close to back to normal behind closed doors. I drifted between phases of being prayer warrior, confused wife, concerned mother, determined partner, and broken woman—and then the anger began to grow. As the years went by, I wondered all the time if that surgeon's cautionary words years ago articulated the root of our problems: the love was missing, and I didn't know if it was hiding deep inside his heart or if it had died on March 11, 2003. I wanted my old life back, but when I shared these feelings, he didn't accept there was a mammoth shift in our life. If half of a couple didn't recognize there was a difference between now and then, how could we put us back together? My family and friends recognized the drastic difference, but the one who mattered most, my husband, did not. I was fighting to control my resentment at losing our beautiful union and constantly questioning the cause of the lack of affection, tenderness, and connection as my husband and I essentially lived as flat mates.

When I posed the question to him, "Do you love me?" and received a faint "Yes," I pulled my caregiver boots back on and tried to focus on my memories of falling in love and the man I married. Yet there were many moments when I wasn't proud of myself; in fact, my father got very honest with me one day over the phone after four years of trying to cope with my new reality. He said, "Anastasia, you are becoming a person you don't want to be." It was the most painful wake-up call. I was blessed with the most loving parents, and I was lashing out even at them. I started to become a person I didn't like looking at in the mirror. I brought those emotions into my office, to my friendships, and it filled the halls in our home. I begged God to tell me what to do, pleaded with my husband to find a way to show me love, and searched for any sign that might tell me how to "push the wheelchair." But I felt like I failed miserably no matter how hard I prayed.

Thankfully, my son kept me motivated, my tribe of soul sisters prevented me from dying inside, I threw myself into work, and, as it always has done for me in the past, music kept me going. Being a part of Richard Lewis's film *August Rush* allowed me to lose myself in music, and as a judge on *Nashville Star* I was able to jump into the dreams of aspiring artists and immerse myself in their talent. I laugh at the nickname contestants gave me, "Simon in a Skirt," as I wonder if I would have stepped into that role without the internal angst created by an accident they knew nothing about. Yet at the end of the day honesty is a rare commodity, so when someone is brave enough to give it, we need to be willing to receive it. The tables were turned for me off the set, as friends started to get honest with me and express concern about my mental well-being. This inspired me to search out help for post-traumatic stress disorder and depression. Eventually, I got out of my deep pit, and I will always appreciate my friends, who were brave enough to speak up and help pull me out.

I still wonder if my spouse knew that he didn't feel the same way about me at some point after the accident but didn't have the heart to tell me, or if his feelings changed because of the trauma of the recovery. The main reason I fell in love with him was because of his ability to love without strings, hold no grudges, and live life with open arms. The extreme difference between us before the accident and after the accident was so radical I didn't know what to do, except reach out to God, family, and best friends. That is what saved me.

In the summer of 2009, I would have drowned in my own grief tsunami, had my family and friends not become my life preserver. But they didn't just allow me to survive—they helped me become a better person on the other side of great loss. I was struggling with issues facing me as the mother of a teenage son, and feeling the strain between my husband and me intensify without any explanations, when the storm struck: I returned home from work one Friday to an unusually quiet home. There, I found my husband's closet empty and learned from a reporter that he had filed for divorce.

I fell apart like a two-dollar watch. Having had no prior discussions about divorce with my husband or received any marriage 911 calls from him, I didn't have time to prepare my body or mind for this shock, and the panic attacks began. (Here's a tip: it's less painful to cry underwater than grab one too many tissues.) Within an hour, my parents and friends showed up and didn't leave my side. Thank God my mom slept with me that night because when I woke up the next morning and realized that it hadn't been a horrible nightmare and this was my reality, I didn't know how I could ever get out of bed. My life as I knew it for ten years was broken into a million pieces and my dream of keeping those sacred vows forever was erased in a matter of hours.

I'm lucky to have been blessed with unshakable faith and relationships grounded in spirituality. Since I couldn't find answers from my husband, I had to search for them in the Bible;

every morning I would let it open randomly and each time the message I needed to hear on that day would give me hope. A few weeks later, as the despair remained, my girlfriends took it upon themselves to take me away to Isla Mujeres, Mexico, where one of my friends has a home with a pool—and tequila. More important, it was a place where I felt safe and loved. My wonderful friends never stopped listening to my endless questions (which mainly consisted of "Why?" again and again). When I didn't feel pretty or lovable, they convinced me that I was. We prayed out loud together, swam, and even laughed once or twice. At one point I asked my friend who's a songwriter to pen "More Tears Than Tequila," and we had a belly laugh people in Cancún probably heard.

Returning to reality, I've never felt so alone in my life as I did walking into the beautiful home we'd built as a family without greeting my husband or my son, who was away at camp. I didn't know what to do with myself and felt completely frozen until my parents and friends came over. With their help I made it through that evening and the next month, which felt like a year, while still in a confused state. Then, another girlfriend scooped me up and took me to the Mii amo Spa in Sedona, Arizona. There, I had the most amazing experience.

While undergoing a therapeutic water treatment in a warm pool, I was instructed to keep my mind blank, pray, and allow any visions and memories to enter my mind at free will. The instructor encouraged me to embrace all good thoughts, and when painful images entered my mind, choose to let the water take them away. When a good vision, like memories with my son and my family came to mind, she merely twirled me in circles. When a painful memory entered my consciousness, she would push my torso deep into the water to help me release that sorrow. My thoughts were random; after envisioning a pair of doves, the memory of that devastating phone call from a friend in 2003 at midnight and hearing the words, "Get on a plane now, your husband's had a brain injury and we don't think he'll make it" flooded in. I didn't say a word as I was recalling the bad memory, but my therapist felt my pain and gently pushed me deeper into the water to release it. Then images of my son, parents, sister, and Jesus seeped into my thoughts right before a vision of our love-filled wedding, followed by a mental picture of my husband's signature on the divorce papers. Again, I let the water take my pain. On and on it went, until exhaustion took over.

After the treatment, my therapist shared that she felt one deep pain from years ago and a very recent one that she helped me set free. I explained what those experiences were and posed my most perplexing question: "I thought my husband was my soul mate, and soul mates are meant to stay together forever." She quietly responded, "Soul mates aren't always meant to be forever; they are put in our lives to teach us our most important lessons. This one taught you how to love unconditionally, and now he's teaching you how to let go." Hearing these words gave me hope, clarity, and amazingly, an appreciation for what I'd been through.

Since that experience in Arizona, beautiful blessings have begun to pour over my life. One of my best friends introduced me to an amazing man who helped me feel beautiful, sexy, and lovable again. While I didn't think I was ready to meet someone new, my tribe did, and forced an introduction with this gorgeous guy who is athletic, positive, spiritual, hilarious, and a perfect fit for me. My family and friends think that my husband's departure and John's arrival were gifts from God. I think they are correct.

With open arms I dove into work and life again, as a whole new authentic me. The only thing nagging at me was my inability to forgive my ex-husband. Without the opportunity for closure, how could I? Throughout our marriage, I had given him so many chances to share his feelings and explained that I was willing to let go if he didn't feel the love any longer; but instead he left me in such a painful and disrespectful way just when I needed him most. While I could come to terms with the fact that he fell out of love, I couldn't get over his ease in abandoning our vows without discussion, the timing, and his cruel method of leaving. Didn't the memory of our amazing love and the sacrifices made deserve greater kindness and consideration? I prayed every day, bored my tribe with my angst, and batted away annoying memories—good and bad—more often than I wanted.

Then one day, I still don't know when or how it happened, but my thought patterns started to change. The pain didn't get in the way of being an engaged mom, partner, daughter, or friend most of the time; my mind and heart opened up.

My work and my circle of friends began expanding in random and exciting ways, which in turn led to new opportunities for growth I couldn't have imagined. One such event took place in August 2010, when my L.A. tribe invited me to an intimate "Full Moon Circle" ceremony, which took place in an enormous teepee; I didn't know it yet, but finally my search for a way to forgive was about to reach the end of the long and winding road. As we all pledged to maintain privacy and keep all that was shared to ourselves, I must remain brief. However, I can say that it was so powerful that the next day, I was able to email my family and friends the good news: "I forgave him in a teepee!" In that moment of self-created closure, I heard the reverberation of so many friends give a sigh of relief all the way in L.A.

My friend Barbra recently told me, "The pain you have overcome has made you easier to love." Closing that chapter in my life was a challenge of immeasurable magnitude, which can perhaps only be matched by the gratitude I feel toward my son, my parents, my sister, and my chosen family of friends for getting me through that time, helping me still believe in True Love, and avoid becoming completely jaded. I'm still learning lessons about unconditional love, and I continue to turn to the water when times get tough, letting the tides take the bad out and focusing on when the good comes rolling in.

Note to self:

Life is not about navigating smooth
waters all of the time.
It's how we swim back to shore
with the help of our
loving lifeguards that matters.

The One That Got Away

ANDREA J. BUCHANAN

Andrea J. Buchanan is a writer living in Philadelphia. She is the bestselling author of The Daring Book for Girls series and the memoir *Mother Shock*, and the editor of three anthologies: *It's a Boy: Women Writers on Raising Sons; It's a Girl: Women Writers on Raising Daughters;* and *Literary Mama: Reading for the Maternally Inclined*. Before becoming a writer, Andi was a classical pianist. Her last recital was at Carnegie Hall's Weill Recital Hall.

I was fifteen the first time a boy called me on the phone. I'd been working as a babysitter and piano teacher for a family in town whose youngest kids were in elementary school and whose oldest son was just graduating high school. Often, when I was there watching the younger kids, the older boy would show up with a friend of his, a cute, funny high school senior, and the two of them would hang out and tease me, and occasionally convince me to play the piano. One day, the older brother showed up without his cute friend and informed me that his buddy wanted my phone number. My response, of course, was "Why?"

It took a few moments to realize that he wasn't kidding, and that his friend really thought I was someone he wanted to get to know better. Still, I was skeptical, sure this was some kind of practical joke.

I was shy, awkward, bookish, and younger than my high school junior classmates, thanks to having skipped a grade—surely not the kind of girl anyone really wanted to talk to on the phone, and certainly not the kind of girl a smart, seventeen-year-old senior who played in a band and watched *Saturday Night Live* might be interested in. But, on the offchance that it wasn't a prank, I said sure, he could have my number.

And then, unbelievably, he called.

I tell my kids sometimes about the way it was back then, how telephones were, like furniture, things that existed only inside the house; how normal it was to answer the phone and have no way of knowing who might be on the other end of the line; how the phone was stuck to the wall, with a long curly cord that stretched, but not really far enough for any true kind of privacy. When Paul called that first time, and I heard my mother answer, sounding incredulous that it was a boy calling for me and not my sister, my stomach leaped into my throat and I unwound the cord as far as it could go, stretching it taut across the kitchen counters, around the doorway, and into the laundry room, as far away as I could get from the curious ears of my family. I huddled in the dark, cradling the plastic orange phone, and listened as this smart, cute, funny guy talked. To me. Of all people.

My teeth chattered, I was so nervous, as he talked to me

about books and music—I remember marveling that he was actually talking to me about books and music—and then before I even realized what was happening, he was asking if we could go out sometime. On a date. My first date. Before I said yes, I asked if he was serious, still suspecting some kind of mean-spirited bet. He laughed and said, "I think you're awesome. This isn't a joke. I promise."

We made plans to spend Saturday at the Zoo and then grab dinner on the way home—a totally acceptable first date, according to my friends, whom I had of course called immediately upon concluding my conversation with Paul. When the big day finally arrived, I agonized over what to wear, but in the end, since it was 1987, I ended up wearing what I usually wore: leggings with a giant shirt, the shoulders of which, naturally, contained enough padding to outfit me as a linebacker. I was nervous when he picked me up, but once we started driving, we started talking, and once we started talking, we started joking, and the witty banter put me at ease. Dating I wasn't so sure about, but funny I could do. At fifteen, funny was pretty much all I had.

But then we got to the Zoo, and when we bought our tickets, it happened: the ultimate in humiliation. The ticket taker looked at Paul and then at me, and then back at Paul, and finally asked: "One adult and one child?"

We were both confused, and then embarrassed as we realized what was going on. The ticket guy had assumed *Paul was the adult and I was the child.* Paul gave him a funny look and said, "No, actually, it's two adults. We're on a date!" Although I was thankful for Paul's attempt at clarification, I was mortified. It's true that at fifteen, I was well under five feet tall and weighed in the neighborhood of eighty-five pounds, but it's also true that at fifteen and on my first date, I didn't want anyone to be pointing out how, well, unwomanly I was.

The ticket incident cast a pall over the rest of the afternoon, feeding into all of my insecurities, and sparking some new ones I hadn't even considered until then. Paul joked about taking me to the children's zoo, but his attempts at humor barely soothed my embarrassment. When we rode the Skyfari and he tried to put his arm around me, I deflected, citing jokey laws about hugging minors. Surely, I thought, he was just trying to make me feel better, a pitying arm-across-the-shoulder move. Surely the ticket guy's comment had given him cause to consider that maybe I was more like a little sister than a romantic interest. My teeth chattered again like they had during our first phone call and I moved to sit across from him on the Skyfari, looking down at all the tiny people below us, wrapping my arms around myself as I tried not to think about how awful it all was.

Things did not improve after the Zoo. At dinner, I was handed the children's menu. Again, Paul was gentlemanly; he flagged down the waitress to request his own pack of crayons, and we had fun making the best of it, coloring in the childish pictures. But I wanted to die inside, just a little bit.

He brought me home and gave me a hug goodbye. I broke free of it before it could possibly morph into anything else and ran inside the house to cry in private. What a disaster, I thought. How could I have actually believed I was a dateable person? I kept most of the shameful facts of our date to myself, telling my friends only that he had been cute and funny and that I was a huge dork so he probably wouldn't call me ever again.

But, to my surprise, he did. This time for a movie. A nighttime date. This did, indeed, seem like the big time—not a little-sister date in broad daylight, but a real, honest-to-goodness, going-out-at-night-like-grown-ups kind of date.

I was terrified.

The thing about terror on a date is that it's difficult to contain. My insecurity and preemptive embarrassment seeped into every interaction we had that night, rendering everything fraught and horrible. At the movie theater, he avoided the "one adult, one child?" question that was of course hanging over my head by announcing to the ticket person and everyone around us that he would like to purchase two adult tickets for two adults who were totally on a date. Which was admirable and funny, but in my heightened state of anticipatory humiliation only served to remind me of the fact that I was not, in fact, an adult; I was a teenager who'd only been on one date in her life and had never been kissed, and what would happen if he actually kissed me, and what if I was no good at it, and what if he didn't like me anymore?

But, even putting those theoretical hyperventilatory questions aside, there was the more practical matter of the movie itself—for he had let me choose the movie, and I of course chose the worst movie in the history of movies. (If you must know: *Mannequin*.) Fifteen minutes in, I knew it was bad. Thirty minutes in, he was actively teasing me about how bad it was. An hour in, and I was positive I had ruined any chance of the night ever turning out okay, thanks to my bad taste.

As we left the theater, he said, mock-sternly, "Well, Amanda, that is the *last* time I let you pick our evening entertainment!"

I was momentarily shocked out of my burgeoning shame. "What did you call me?"

"Amanda," he said, seeming slightly bemused. "That is your actual name, right?"

"Uh, no," I told him. "It's Andrea. Andi is a nickname for Andrea."

"Huh," he said. "I totally thought it was Amanda. Okay, Andrea it is!"

He proceeded to walk me to the car as if the whole evening—my stupid movie choice, his misunderstanding of my real name—was no big deal, but I was in a daze. Suddenly it all made sense to me: he had no idea who I really was. He had been trying to date some fancy version of me, who of course did not exist. He thought I was Amanda, a grown-up adult; but I was just me, Andi, this scrawny, inexperienced child.

My humiliation had seemed so thorough that when he took me home, I was sure it couldn't get any worse. But it did: he walked me to the door and met my mom. My mom, who invited him in. My mom, who proceeded to flirt with him. My mom, who acted like I wasn't even in the room. My mom, who acted like *she* was on a date. My mom, who invited him to come for dinner "any time" and even suggested she get out her guitar so they could "jam." Again, Paul was polite and held his own in what had to be an obviously weird situation (even when I blurted out, "God, mom, why don't *you* go out with him next time!"). But I felt like a huge romantic failure—a sense that was only magnified when I walked him back to his car and he went in for the kiss. Because as he leaned in close, all I could think about was the children's menu and the crayons and *Mannequin* and Amanda and my flirty mom, and I just panicked.

"You know my mom's probably totally watching us," I said, easing away from him. "We should probably just shake hands."

And then I mumbled something about it being against the law or something to kiss your little sister, and I fled.

I lay in bed that night replaying every awful moment for shame-maximizing purposes. I wished I could have been Amanda—I *should* have been Amanda! Amanda would have picked the right movie; Amanda would have been tall and womanly; Amanda would never be mistaken for a child; Amanda would totally know what to do on a date. Amanda would never panic and run.

I will spare you the details of how it all gradually unraveled, how I made the mistake of telling a gossipy friend the truth about what had happened, how the news got back to Paul in a very public way that I had told someone about how we hadn't kissed; how he and his friend seemed to avoid me at my baby-sitting gigs, how soon he began calling me less and less.

One afternoon, I called him, my teeth chattering like crazy, and asked him if he might want to go to my school's carnival night with me, and he said, "I can't. I'm really busy. With my band and stuff. And actually, I don't think I want to have a girl-friend anymore, so . . ."

"Oh, okay," I said through my chattering teeth. "Um, well, I guess I'll talk to you later?"

He said okay and we hung up the phone, and only then did I realize: *I had been his girlfriend?*

At fifteen I didn't know yet, of course, the heartbreak that awaited me. And I mean this in the most literal sense: I couldn't anticipate the various ways, from the mundane to the profound, in which life would break my heart open in years to come. The troubled, charismatic, musical genius boyfriend who stunted me in music school; the isolation and loneliness of coping with a mysterious illness that dragged on for years; the stress and exhilaration of career successes and failures; the amazing luck of marrying a man who seemed to love me more than I loved even myself; the pain of childbirth—twice—and with that the humbling facts of parenthood: the terrifying depths of depression, the fierce love and confusion, the pure helplessness of watching your children suffer, the fantastical joy of watching your children thrive. I knew none of this. And how could I? I was a teenager. All I knew for sure was that I was fifteen, and I was heartbroken.

Looking back now, with the fondness I might have if I were thinking of this happening to my own daughter, I am glad that, as awful as it felt, this was all it was: the sadness of only realizing after the fact that I had been someone's girlfriend after all. As much as it hurt then, it was, I know now, laughably benign.

But the experience stayed with me. Over the years, every once in a while, I would think back to those few dates with Paul and wonder what became of him. Of all the people I'd met and then lost touch with in my life, he was the one I always returned to in my mind, wishing I could have a second chance to explain myself and resolve all of that adolescent turmoil I didn't have the vocabulary to express back then.

I never imagined that I might actually get my wish.

Almost two decades later, I had three anthologies published within a few months of each other, and in support of those books I took to the Web, doing what at the time was considered a brand-new thing: a blog-based book tour. One hundred or so bloggers wrote about the books, and I wrote about them, too, on the blog I kept at the time; other bloggers hosted interviews with me or wrote entries about their own books that tied into mine. It was a nice way to get the word out, and more than that, it was fun. One blogger in particular, though, asked me a question about dating, hoping I could make a list of what I'd learned from dates I'd had, and I was momentarily stumped. As you know now, from reading thus far, my dating experience was not exactly stellar. In fact, after Paul, I only had maybe five more encounters that could technically even be considered "dates," and then I met my husband and got married. So I wasn't sure what to say.

In the end, I kept it vague, but I did mention Paul, in an oblique way, as being filed under the header of "the one that got away." Well, okay, it wasn't exactly oblique: I mentioned him by his first and quite distinctive last name. Still, as I knew from having Googled him in the process of thinking about my answer, he didn't have much of an online footprint, so it seemed unlikely he would ever come across it.

And he didn't. But someone else did.

Soon after the interview was posted, I got an email from a woman who'd come across the blog entry precisely because she'd been doing the same kind of Googling I'd done, looking to see if Paul had any sort of internet presence. She was an old friend of his who had lost touch, and she was hoping I might be able to provide an email address for him, as she hadn't been able to find one. More than that, though, was a tantalizing bit of information she shared. She said she'd worked with him abroad, teaching English after college, and that he had talked about me.

He. Had talked. About me.

She and I traded a few emails, sharing info and stories about our mutual friend, and then I decided, screw it. Enough with the idle Googling. I was going to go full internet detective and track him down. So I did.

There were actually a few people with his rather unusual name, but I figured he probably wasn't the Paul who was a newly born-again Christian, or the Paul who was an old car enthusiast, or the Paul who was a prominent and prolific eBay seller. Not that he couldn't have been any of those Pauls; it just seemed more likely that he was the Paul who had released a few indie CDs in the nineties and now worked as a teacher. I wrote to the email address I was able to track down, my teeth chattering a little bit for old time's sake as I nervously hit send: *Hello. I don't know if this is the right Paul, but perhaps you might remember me. We went on a few dates in high school—I played the piano and was a total dork. If any of that rings a bell, let me know—an old friend of yours contacted me hoping to get in touch with you, and asked me to pass her email address along if I found you!*

A few days later, I had a reply. I had indeed contacted the right Paul, and he did indeed remember me—with one glaring discrepancy. He did not remember me as being a dork, he wrote. He remembered me as being a cool, awesome, talented girl who he was stupid enough to let get away.

I was "the one that got away"? That couldn't be possible. How could that be possible? For years after our pathetic nonrelationship, I had regretted my inexperience and lack of appeal, wondering if I could ever bridge the gap between insecure, unsure Andi and this confident Amanda person I *should* be in order to be truly dateable. For years I had thought of myself as somehow romantically defective, and even though I'd managed to grow into some kind of positivity and acceptance as an adult,

I still carried a little bit of that awkward, ugly-duckling sense of myself inside me.

But if *I* was "the one that got away"—if *I* had been the cool one, the intimidating one, the awesome one—that meant I had spent years laboring under a delusion. That meant I had spent years hiding in the shadows, keeping myself safe by thinking I had limits, never risking vulnerability. That meant I had spent years thinking of myself one way when I could have just as easily thought of myself another. That meant I had spent years being . . . wrong?

Paul and I struck up a brief correspondence, trading memories via email and having the kind of conversation twenty years later that we never could have had as teenagers, standing outside my house as he prepared to drive away, my mom's shadow darkening the window, the dewy grass glistening in the moonlight, a chill in the air. I told him what it had been like for me (he was awesome, I was nervous, I'd felt like I wasn't good enough), and he told me what it had been like for him (*I* was awesome, *he* was nervous, *he'd* felt like *he* wasn't good enough). It wasn't so much rewriting history as it was explaining it, with the benefit of hearing both sides of the story, from folks who were a bit wiser and had more perspective than the original participants. An actual real-life example of a concept I'd heard but always suspected was imaginary, a psychological unicorn: *closure*.

I wished I could go back in time to visit fifteen-year-old me, on one of those nights, any of those nights, when I wrote in my journal, heartbroken over Paul, wondering if I would ever kiss or be kissed by anyone, and tell her what I'd learned: That everything was going to turn out fine, that she would go places and accomplish things she couldn't even imagine, that she would indeed find love and be loved. But most of all that she was beautiful, and that she didn't need to be anyone except the person she was already becoming.

It wasn't exactly time travel, but writing those emails and reading his responses was a little bit like that: a postcard from the present to the fifteen-year-old girl from the past who still lived, however faintly, inside me.

My email correspondence with Paul bloomed and then withered, running its course as we caught up with one another, marveled at our teenaged selves, and then eventually moved on with our lives. I told my husband the story of our reconnecting, and how strange it was to realize that I could have let go of that image of myself as a dorky loser years before, at any point along the way. (Having heard the story of my dates with Paul, he immediately joked, "Wait, was this the *Mannequin* guy? And he forgave you for picking that movie?") The last I heard from Paul, he had moved back to our old hometown and was teaching there, starting a family.

I no longer ruminate about that teenaged time in my life, wishing desperately for an "undo" command that could erase those uncomfortable moments as easily as I can backspace and delete in an email today. The mythical Amanda—the notion that there was some sophisticated version of me that I really ought to be but wasn't—no longer haunts me. And what grown-up me knows now that fifteen-year-old me couldn't, for whatever reason, is that I can choose to think of myself and those around me—the situations I am in and the motivations of people I interact with—in the best possible light, *at any time, whenever I want.* I don't have to wait twenty years to have perspective and proof that I am really okay: I can decide that for myself, right now.

Because I know that the truth is that it wasn't really Paul who was the one that got away. It was me. Even though I had been right there all along.

> *Note to self:*
>
> **Closure at its best is both an ending and a beginning.**

Sixty and Single

ANDREA CAGAN

Andrea Cagan is an author, editor, and collaborator who has brought a dozen books to the bestseller lists over the past two decades. Previously a member of the Harkness Ballet Company in New York, she currently lives in Los Angeles with her Balinese cat, Lulu.

I always imagined that life as a single person would be horrible, because it would mean that a big part of what I'd always envisioned my future would hold would be missing, and therefore I would feel unfulfilled. The fear of this actually happening paralyzed me. However, as I am now about to enter my sixty-second year on this planet, that fear has become a reality, but the imagined consequences have turned out to be far from true. Listen up, ladies: I am single *and* happy. Shocking, I know.

Trust me, I haven't always been this way. I was born hardwired to be in a relationship. I come from a loving family in which my mother was happily married to my father for fifty-one years. Despite the fact that they bickered like all married people do, they had a wonderful marriage, and they undoubtedly functioned as a unit. They were a strong example, and for most of my life I was a serial monogamist.

I got married to my first husband when I was nineteen years old—way too young to know better. I was a professional ballet dancer at the time and he was my first real boyfriend. I dated him for about a year, I didn't really know how to be in the world alone, and when he said he wanted to get married, I said okay because saying no and being on my own was just too scary. I remember being engaged even though I really didn't want to get married, and figuring, *Oh well, that's just what you do.* So I did. I left the ballet and stayed married for seven years, which was six years and 364 days longer than I should've. There were a lot of drugs involved in our shared life, and the marriage deteriorated into a physically abusive relationship in the end. It was a big mess. After years of wanting to leave him but not having the courage, one day I'd finally had enough and I fled the scene. A guy I knew hid me in his houseboat in Marin County so my husband wouldn't find me and I kept my whereabouts a secret from just about everyone, even my family, because I knew if my spouse found out, he would come and get me. It was a terrifying time.

Finally, after a few weeks, I got up the courage to go back to the house I'd shared with my husband and gather my things when I assumed he'd be out. Unfortunately, my timing was off, and he was there. When he saw me, he became so enraged, he beat me up. I left without a single possession and never looked back. For years, well after our divorce, every time I heard his name I felt fear. He invaded my dreams, and it took me a long time to stop looking behind me when I was walking down a street, much less trust a man. Eventually, I got into therapy, off drugs, and regained the courage to get back out into the world.

My next few relationships were with men who were on the docile side. In retrospect, I guess they could be considered a little wimpy, but they were nice and gentle, which is what I required because I wanted to make sure if I had a fight, I could win.

As these relationships played out, I was finding my writing voice and traveling the world. I had lived in Europe when I was a professional ballet dancer, and was comfortable with living abroad. When I started to write, I became passionate about the Philippine Faith Healers; I traveled to Asia about ten times to follow the psychic surgeons, and I wrote my first book, *Awakening the Healer Within*, about them. It was published twenty years ago, when nobody was awakening anything within yet, and certainly not writing about it. Then everybody started awakening everything and I became a little turned off by the mainstream treatment of the topic, so I found other subjects and people to write about. I've been very lucky in following my passions, working very hard, and making a really nice living this way.

While my involvement in my work came easy to me, finding love eluded me at every turn. Sure, I had some really nice relationships during my thirties, but nothing that stuck. Some relationships ended because I made more money and had more success than the man I was with. And there's no doubt that my first marriage wounded me deeply, and even though I worked at trying to heal the scars, there was always this deep-seated fear that kept me from truly trusting another man, diving in deep and giving myself over to the sublime pleasure of pure vulnerability and commitment.

Then, one day, when I was forty-five years old, my luck—actually, I think it was my heart—changed. It opened. Okay, it burst. I was hanging out at a friend's house in Venice, California, when a young man (seventeen years younger than I, to be exact) walked in and the dam broke. He was English, and he had a really nice body and a gleam in his eye that was part youthfulness and part mischievous. Our attraction to one another was powerful from the moment we met. May–December romances had never been my thing—sure, I'd dated men who were a little younger, but I'd never dated a man *that* much younger than me—but when that lightning bolt of desire and recognition strikes, all of our pretenses and preconceptions about what something should look like take a backseat to feelings, and feelings win over.

I discovered that, along with the instant spark and irresistible attraction, there was an added bonus in being with someone so much younger. I'd been feeling stuck in my ways and I found my new lover's youth and zest for life very interesting, and very fun. The sex was wonderful—not the greatest I ever had, but I really enjoyed it. The amazing thing was, by being with him, there was some part of me that woke up to the woman I had been twenty years earlier, where things felt possible and fresh. I had that feeling from the moment I met him and I loved it.

About two years into our relationship, his visa expired. I desperately wanted him to stay in the States, so we did what so many couples in similar situations have to do, and got hitched. I wasn't sure if we would grow old together. Actually, I wasn't sure how *any* of it would work. I knew it might fall apart, but I was really hoping it would last, and there was only one way to find out.

It did last—for about two years. Eventually, our age difference created a void between us that was impossible to fill. We were in sync physically, but emotionally we were worlds apart. While he was still searching for a career, uncertain of who he wanted to be when he grew up, my career was taking off in a big way. I had just gotten my largest paycheck ever for writing a book, and he, like men I'd dated before, was intimidated by that and started to shut down. He became more and more distant until I felt like I was alone in my own house even when he was sitting right next to me.

Around this time, my husband became attached to a woman his own age who he met at the gym where we worked out. I asked him if they were involved romantically and he said, no, they were just close friends, but it still didn't sit well with me. Everything came to a head after we were married for a year. He had gotten more and more removed until I gave him an ultimatum: "You either need to be present in this relationship or go." And so he went. I was forty-nine years old.

This might sound like a really crappy ending to a lovely relationship, and it was. But it was also the beginning of a major life transformation. For one thing, it was the only relationship in my life where I didn't have anyone waiting in the wings. (Usually I had a foot out the door before things really fell apart. I've never been a cheater, but I tend to begin the process of moving on early and sometimes overlap occurs). And secondly, the part of me that was awakened by that relationship never went back to sleep.

On the morning of my fiftieth birthday, I felt more lonely than ever before. I was at the prime of my life and wanted to find someone to share it with. But no men were calling, and I had no prospects. So I took off to see a close girlfriend in Hawaii shortly after my birthday. When I returned to Los Angeles with the usual spring in my step, I decided to give dating one more shot. I went on a few fix-ups and to a couple of parties, and I even had a few romances here and there, but at the end of each evening, I couldn't wait to get home and hang out with my cats.

It took me about a year to get through the beating-myself-up-for-being-alone phase, and then it started to dawn on me that if I couldn't wait to get home and be alone, then maybe being alone wasn't such a bad thing after all. If being with a man was less interesting than being alone, why would I want to be with him? That became my criterion for determining whether I should go on a date with someone, and soon I stopped going out . . . *with men.*

I started going out more with my girlfriends and really fostering my female relationships. I've always had a wealth of women in my life, and without them I don't know where I would be. They have always been there for me when I was confused, vulnerable, or in need of nurturing, and I have been there for them in return.

I now have a smart, dynamic, caring set of friends I can call on to have fun with and address any emotional needs I might be experiencing. I also have a very close relationship with my girlfriend who lives in Hawaii who is in a similar situation to me right now in terms of our love lives. Our relationship is completely about support and nurturing. Our rhythms are similar, and we talk every day, sometimes spending hours going over all of our day-to-day dramas together and working things out. We don't lie in bed and hug or kiss like a romantic couple (I'm not a lesbian, and neither is she), but we giggle and love each other and it fills me up.

Getting to this place wasn't easy. I used to doubt myself and wonder why I wasn't coming home to a man who could fix things, spoon me, and take care of the chores I hate to do. I figured there had to be something wrong with me. But little by little, I realized that the real issue was that I needed to undo the belief that someone else was supposed to take care of me. When I came to that conclusion, I stopped giving myself a hard time.

I may have let myself off the hook, but I wasn't the only one questioning my choices. I can't count the times I've been accosted by women my age at parties when they find out I'm single and I'm fine with it. It's as if they go into hyper drive, emphatically shaking their fingers in my face and telling me, "You're too pretty, you have to find a man," or, "You're such a catch, I just don't get it," or my favorite line, "You gotta get a man or you'll end up alone with cats, knitting." When I hear that, I always think, *But I love my cats and I love to knit. Does this mean I've failed?*

Then I typically take a sip of wine, eat a cheese cube, and walk away. And I find the answer within myself: No, I haven't failed. I never imagined being single and sixty, but I feel more love around me now than I ever felt.

My life has illuminated itself in a brilliant way. It's taken a lot of work, some false moves, and a depth of understanding and patience with myself to get to this point, but I have a wealth of joy that as a young woman, I never felt and didn't know existed. And the fear that gripped me as I was either running from an abusive relationship or running into a dysfunctional one is gone. I'm alone and I love it. In fact, I'm alone and I love me.

Note to self:

**One is the loneliest number,
but it can also be the most abundant.**

My First Love

TAMIKA CATCHINGS

Tamika Catchings is a professional basketball player for the WNBA's Indiana Fever and has spent several seasons playing internationally in South Korea, Poland, Russia, and Turkey. After playing at Adlai E. Stevenson High School and graduating from Duncanville High School in Texas, Catchings became one of the stars of the University of Tennessee women's basketball team. In 2001, she was drafted by the Indiana Fever. After sitting out her rookie year due to injury, she had an all-star rookie season in 2002. She is a six-time WNBA All-Star, a seven-time All-WNBA recipient, a two-time Olympic Gold Medalist, and has been named Defensive Player of the Year four times. Catchings is also the founder of the Catch the Stars Foundation, which empowers youth through sports.

*M*y first love was not a boy named Michael, or a guy named Tom. He didn't buy me flowers or take me to the movies or write me love notes in math class. My first love happened on a court, between two hoops, and involved a stylish yet sophisticated swoosh named Niké and a smooth, handsome ball named Spalding.

I have always considered basketball to be my first love, not just because I live it, breathe it, and make my living playing it, but because the court is where I learned self-confidence and empowerment, and where I first realized that I could do and be anything my heart desired.

It's where I learned to love myself.

I was born with basketball in my blood. My father, Harvey Catchings, played in the NBA for eleven seasons. But as a little kid, I was probably the last person you'd expect to become a star on any court. I was born with a moderate hearing impairment that impacted me greatly as a young girl. Not only did I have to wear hearing aids, my speech was also affected by my hearing loss. On top of all that, I wore glasses and was one of the tallest kids in my class as far back as I can remember. Long story short, I was a prime target for kids' cruelty, and I spent much of my elementary and junior high school years getting teased by my peers. It was not a fun time for me, and it certainly wasn't good for my self-esteem. I never felt pretty. I just felt different.

Around second grade, I started becoming involved in sports. I remember feeling good about myself during games, like I was on top of the world. Thanks to countless days of practice, I became good enough that the boys would choose me for their teams over the other guys, and I started to hang out with the boys so that I could play ball. For me, boys represented sports competition, and I had no problem whatsoever going one-on-one with any of them. I certainly didn't have any other agenda with guys, unlike the other girls at the time. While they were buying new outfits to attract the attention of the boys, I was buying new sneakers so that I could run faster than them on the court.

It wasn't until the summer before I started high school that a light bulb went on in my head, and I began to think of a certain boy as more than just a great friend; all of a sudden, I remember thinking that he was cute—real cute. And as luck would have it, he was a little bit taller than me. We played lots of ball together, and I would let him win every once in a while. We also started going on dates, and soon we officially became an item. Basketball was still my first love, but no longer my only love.

That relationship didn't last, but when it ended, my first love was still there for me, as was my support system: my grandparents. Throughout my life, I moved around a lot; between my father's basketball career, and the fact that my parents got divorced when I was in sixth grade, I split my time between my mom and dad's houses. My grandparents on both sides were a constant source of stability and inspiration to me; they taught me what love can do and how it can stand the test of time. Even in their darkest hours—battling cancer, surviving strokes, seeing their spouse pass away—there was a sense of peace about them because their love was so strong. I've now lost both my grandfathers and my grandmother on my father's side, but what I haven't lost is the strong urge to emulate what they had: a long-lasting commitment to one another, until death did them part.

Finding the kind of love my grandparents shared has not been as easy as I'd have liked it to be. I have no illusion that meeting someone and staying together is a walk in the park. My lifestyle is such that I'm on the road for months out of the year, playing basketball for the WNBA, giving speeches, and showing up at events and appearances; and during the off season, I play for other teams in other countries. I also started a foundation that aspires to empower young people by getting them involved in sports, so my life is very full. It takes a certain kind of man not to feel intimidated by me. Not just because I'm six feet one but because I'm fully engaged in my life and want to be the best at everything I do. Always.

While I don't want anyone to feel intimidated by me, I also can accept nothing less than someone's full respect. Women in sports have come a long way thanks to Title IX, the federal law passed in 1972 which states that "No person in the United States shall, on the basis of sex, be excluded from participation in, be denied the benefits of, or be subjected to discrimination under any education program." It was this law that paved the way for women to participate in athletics in schools. But even so, I think there's still an unspoken sexism that permeates our society around female athletes in general, and especially professional female athletes. It's something I have to deal with every day, so I have to pick and choose the guys that I'm going to go out with carefully.

For the most part, I've been lucky. I've been fortunate enough to date some great guys that really get me, even if they just haven't been "the one." I'm still searching for someone who can give me the kind of love that empowers me, fulfills me, and serves God at the same time, and I pray that when it's the right moment, and the right person, I'll be able to recognize it.

Until then, I have basketball.

I find so much joy, and a deep sense of commitment and familiarity, whenever I run out onto a court. Whether I'm playing in front of thousands of screaming fans, or in a high school gym trying to inspire kids, between those two hoops, running with Niké and dribbling with Spalding, I am, after all these years, still head over heels in love.

Note to self:

If you find *what* you love
as well as *who* you love,
that's a perfect life.

The Romance of
Making It Through Unscathed

KELLY CORRIGAN

Kelly Corrigan is the author of *The Middle Place*, which spent six months on the *New York Times* Best Sellers list. Her second book, *Lift*, debuted at #2. She has been called "the poet laureate of the ordinary." Kelly and her family live in Northern California.

I was raised—as girls were, as girls still are—with princesses and fairy tales and soundtracks that make me tear up even today. I spent a lot of time in dress-ups, pulling together pink boas and clacking high heels and sparkly plastic earrings, then taking the whole fantastic ensemble slowly down the stairs to show my mom and dad, who would tilt their heads to the side and aww. If it was after five, and my parents' friends were over cocktailing, I could get a whole room of infused adults to validate my princessness. Mrs. Burch would say I was perfect, Mr. Maroney would fall to his knee and propose, Mrs. Moran would tell me I had Snow White beat.

Eventually, at an appropriate age, I abandoned dress-ups.

But I did not abandon the idea that something terribly romantic was in store for me.

In my twenties, I moved to San Francisco, where the streets are littered with sporty Prince Charmings in fleece pullovers. I was also coming of age with the internet, back when Henry Blodget claimed Amazon would sell for $400 a share and then in no time at all, Amazon's stock price went to $425. Remember those first mouth-watering whiffs of preposterous riches? Me, too. So the ball gown and the staircase, the orchestra and the scurrying staff, these things seemed less and less fairy-tale-ish.

I had been going to weddings for nearly a decade when, finally, I found a keeper, right there in the kitchen of my friend's house, pouring himself a glass of Merlot and offering to refill mine. After some saucy how-ya-doing, he told me that he had just taken a job with Teleworld, in the Valley. Teleworld, he explained, was going to change television forever, and he was the twenty-eighth employee. He bought his stock options on his first day, for four cents apiece.

It was in this time of great expectations that I was made weak and rosy-cheeked by my last first kiss ever. It was June and the car top was down. Within a year, I became a wife, Teleworld became TiVo, and checking our options became an aphrodisiac. From what I could see, those old fairy tales had turned into a working road map. My terribly romantic and dramatic something was at hand.

It shames me to admit what I thought that *something* might be, but, for sure, it included an interior decorator, a personal chef, and commissioned artwork in the foyer. It also included four kids who all kinda looked alike and palled around together like Kennedys.

Then, one Thursday night, my brand-new husband totaled his brand-new car on the way home from an IPO meeting at TiVo. He was unharmed but electric with shock. Not much later, a friend delivered an eight-pound baby girl, stillborn at forty weeks. And I found a seven-centimeter tumor in my breast one night while taking a bubble bath with my two little girls who don't look alike and have twenty-some fights a day.

Oh.

Now, the fantasy is this: Me in a living room that I decorated myself with a couch from Pottery Barn, a bookcase from IKEA, and a painting my sister-in-law did. I am eighty. I am opening the mail and out fall snapshots of my grandchildren riding bikes or ice-skating or just sitting there looking like your basic normal, healthy kids. And Edward, my last first kiss ever, is still there, still sitting next to me.

Note to self:

It's a rare thing to get from one
end of your life to the other
without tragedy.
So that means you need to keep
reminding yourself of two things:
when crisis hits,
somehow you'll survive;
and if crisis doesn't hit,
you're awfully lucky.

The Quiet Room

JESSICA CUSHMAN

Jessica Cushman, a former actress and future writer, works as an architectural designer in Los Angeles. Born in Switzerland and raised internationally, she now lives in La Canada, California, with her husband, toddler, and wonderful stepkids. She is currently writing a book about her experience with postpartum depression.

I wish I could have known, somehow, that it would all turn out okay. That after rocketing from being single and alone at thirty-nine, to meeting my future husband, to getting pregnant right away and then having the most beautiful baby, only to end up back in the hospital soon after—the psych ward this time—for postpartum depression so bad my husband feared for my life and, in truth, so did I . . . that after *all* of that, I'd still be okay.

But I didn't know that. Not yet.

There wasn't only sadness or blackness or anxiety in those early months. I was madly in love with my baby from the beginning and there was much joy, fascination, wonder, and excitement, too. Yet as the exhaustion crept up after weeks of sleeplessness, the adrenaline high that had kept me going all those days and nights started swirling into a crippling anxiety that almost killed me. It all ended up being a gift. All of it. But I could never have known this at the time.

If I had to take a guess at what put me in the psych ward of the hospital, I'd have to say it's that it all happened much too fast. I met my future husband, and after only six weeks we bought and renovated a house. Over the next year and a half, I got pregnant, eloped, became a stepmother, and had a baby.

It was a lot.

When I met Paul, something in me immediately said yes. This silver thread of energy ran through my belly when he held me, telling me to take the plunge. Everything moved into fast-forward with us right from the start. The house we bought after just over a month of dating needed a massive renovation that stretched out over the next six months; it was a big test of our relationship, but it was nothing compared to what was coming.

We stopped using birth control early on, as I was forty and knew time was of the essence. So I was surprised when I got pregnant pretty much right away. At my ten-week checkup, we stared into the black monitor with its white otherworldly shadows and saw a tiny, fluttering motion. A heartbeat. These cells were making a heart. It was astounding and deeply moving, and I found myself crying in a mixture of relief and awe that there was another heart flickering to life inside of me. It was real—we were going to have a baby.

A couple weeks before our daughter was due, Paul and I buckled on our decision to wait to get married until the summer after the baby was born. Suddenly, getting married before she arrived felt like the right thing to do. So, without telling anyone, we jumped on a boat and went out to Catalina, just twenty miles off the coast of Southern California, where we lived, and got married at City Hall for $72. Afterwards, we got a huge double strawberry ice cream cone as our symbolic wedding cake. We vowed not to tell anyone, since we still planned to have a "real" wedding that summer and didn't want to spoil it.

Days later, it was time to go to the hospital. To say that the birth was traumatic doesn't really cover it; I was in labor for forty-one hours. The epidural wore off by the time I delivered, and I needed ten stitches from the tearing. On top of that, the placenta didn't all deliver so I needed a manual retrieval. I was screaming so loudly it terrified everyone on the floor. I was pleading with Paul and anyone who would listen to make it stop, but to no avail. I would have flashbacks of this for months to come, and each time it would reduce me to tears and leave me shaking.

But in some ways, the birth experience was also extraordinary. It really is a life and death struggle, and you can't quite imagine the power of it until you've actually gone through it. It bonded me to Paul in a way I could never have imagined. He was everything to me in that delivery room, and it locked us together for life. And seeing our daughter, Tessa's, face for the first time is the greatest miracle I've ever known. My love for her caught flame that instant and has grown ever since.

Soon after she was born, however, things started to fall apart. I was in more pain breastfeeding than I ever thought possible, and had to use the same pain management techniques

I'd learned to get through labor contractions. But this was only the beginning of my frantic struggle to stay afloat while feeling like I had no idea what I was doing or how to do it.

I was struck again and again by the intense vulnerability of a baby, of *my* baby. They have no defenses. None. Not even an awareness of danger or threat, much less an ability to ward it off or report on it. She had no protection, no shell. I remember responding to someone who asked how "wonderful" it was to have a baby that it was more like someone had sliced me open and taken out all my internal organs, put them on a tray, given them back to me to take care of, and then left me alone to figure it all out. But the fearful thoughts were equally matched by the bliss. The tenderness and love that enveloped me as I held that baby was unlike anything I'd ever known.

On the fourth day after her birth, we took her back to the doctor for a mandatory checkup due to jaundice. The doctor said that she was getting such a small amount of milk from me that her body was starting to shut down from dehydration and malnutrition, which is why she was so tired and sleepy all the time. I was flooded with dread that my instincts could be so wrong. We gave her her first bottle right then and there in the doctor's office and, sure enough, she gulped the entire thing down in about ten seconds.

I was told to continue breastfeeding while we supplemented with formula, and that soon enough my milk would come in, but it continued to be very problematic. Finally, my OB prescribed a drug that boosted milk supply. This doubled my output, which only meant it went from one ounce to two. What the OB didn't tell me was that this drug also tends to heighten anxiety. Given that I was already shooting back and forth between bliss and panic, I don't know that I should have been taking drugs that further rocked my emotional stability.

I don't know exactly how to explain why my stress levels were suddenly so high, except that everything in my life had changed in the past year and I felt I had no solid footing. I'd never lived with anyone before, ever. I'd never been married; I'd never had kids; I'd never had stepkids; I'd never lived in my new town; I'd certainly never had a baby or even really cared for one by myself. I was in the deep end of the pool, and after only a month, I was starting to feel like I was drowning.

My family all came out, one by one, to help that first month. Their tenderness and care was so generous, and I needed them so much. But when the last of them had come and gone, I felt such loss. I had learned so many vital things from them about how to burp and wrap and hold and change and comfort Tessa. As I stood at the doorway and waved goodbye, I felt utterly alone.

It was right around week five that the panic started to set in. I had become exhausted and was running out of anything to give. Even more problematic was that I felt I couldn't show it. I was supposed to know how to do this; I was supposed to be good at this; I was supposed to be in love not only with Tessa, but with my new husband and my new life and my new stepkids and my new town and my new house and all of it. But more and more, all I was feeling was tired, and the source of my exhaustion was not going anywhere. I had set myself up for sink or swim, and I was starting to sink.

What had been fairly limited to a daytime sleep problem started becoming a nighttime problem that week. When I lay down, my heart would start racing. Every minute that ticked by seemed the most precious of minutes lost, and the level of deadening fatigue just kept climbing. It would take me an hour to finally drift off, and fifteen minutes later Tessa would be up for another feeding. I would awaken in the early morning to her crying, and the pleading my body would do for more sleep was so intense it made me understand why sleep deprivation torture works.

The first month there had been a kind of elation, but soon my body just started to shut down. I had started weeping while I was nursing Tessa. My head would drop down from total, mind-numbing fatigue as I held her to my breast, and when she was done, I'd give her the bottle too, praying that she would fall asleep, rocking her until her eyelids drooped before putting her in her crib. Afterwards, I had to pump for thirty minutes to try and get my milk supply up. Then I would finally fall into our bed and, inexplicably, still not be able to fall asleep.

I could see that Paul was getting worried about me, and I thought I saw disappointment, too. *Moms all over the world breastfeed every day*, I thought. *I should be able to as well.*

Paul was suffering, too. He was missing his other kids, who were staying at his ex-wife's house for three months to give us time to adjust to having a new baby. He was also trying to cope at his new demanding job, while trying to help me when he could, and the feedings in the middle of the night were waking him up as well. He wasn't as sleep-deprived as I was, but he was suffering.

I needed help. I was sinking and I knew it. I could feel despair closing in on me. I loved this little baby with everything I had, but I felt like I was starting to die from lack of sleep. I dug through an old book on pregnancy that someone gave me and looked up insomnia. It was then that I learned that postpartum depression (PPD) can also manifest itself in anxiety attacks. I thought it was only sadness or despair, but now I saw that I was having all the classic symptoms.

Earlier that week, I'd seen a woman at my breastfeeding support group who was playing with her baby, just giggling and enjoying her little girl. This was so far from where I was emotionally, the contrast became immediately clear to me. Whatever vital and important nutrients Tessa was getting from the miracle of breast milk was going to pale in comparison to the unhappy, joyless mother I was rapidly becoming.

I was afraid to tell Paul that I might have PPD, but I did so that night. He was supportive and willing to do whatever I wanted or needed him to do. I also told him I was going to stop breastfeeding, and I think he was relieved to see the end of the torture I was going through. But I was devastated and felt like a failure, even as I knew it had to stop. The bonding and the hormones and the nurturing and all the magic that comes with breastfeeding . . . I thought that would all be lost. But I can happily report from the other side of the abyss that it's just not true.

The next morning I called my OB for help with the anxiety and depression and also told her I'd decided to give up breastfeeding. She put me on a birth control pill to stabilize my hormones, which would go wild from weaning, and told me how to bind my breasts to help stop the milk production. Then, over the next forty-eight hours, she also wrote me prescriptions for Ambien CR (a sleep medication) and Ativan (an anti-anxiety medication). She also told me to renew my old prescription for Effexor (an antidepressant) and Xanax (an anti-anxiety medication) that a different doctor had prescribed before my pregnancy for help with my lifelong sleepwalking and some low-grade anxiety. I remember thinking it was all going to be okay now . . . I just needed some sleep and then it would all be okay.

By the next day, I felt freed emotionally from all that tortured, insane trying, trying, trying to breastfeed. I was now a formula-feeding mom and we were going to be just fine. Any minute the Effexor would kick in, the anxiety attacks would go away, and my sleeping would improve. I was going to be okay. Except that I wasn't; I continued having anxiety attacks, and I was still sleeping horribly.

That week, Tessa made a big leap in her sleep durations while I had my first night of official insomnia. I felt like my head was going to explode and I reviewed the same worries again and again, faster and faster. I thought I might implode from anxiety. I knew I had to stop it somehow, so I went on a walk and started naming every single thing I saw to break the cycle. I wasn't allowed to think about anything else—no problem solving, no knots to untie. Just naming things: Rock. Dirt. Fence. Weed. Flower. Cloud. Tree. Bush. Shoe. Hedge. And on and on. It felt crazy, and yet, it worked to a degree. It unhinged my exhausted brain for half an hour.

But as the days wore on and I got less and less sleep, the drive to fall asleep hit desperate levels. I hired some young girls to come in for a few hours each day to give me relief from baby duty, but having to teach them how to help often made my anxiety worse. I set up the guest room with blackout curtains as a place to try and force some sleep in the day. There, the world was snuffed out with earplugs and an eye mask in the hope that sleep might suddenly descend and whisk me away. It never did. These long hours of trying but failing to sleep brought only more despair, fear, anxiety, and, now, a roaring throb in my limbs that demanded I move or rub them every few minutes.

I was heading into the week that brought me to the edge. Tessa was seven weeks old.

A few days later, I stopped being able to sleep at all. I also lost my ability to eat, and the medications—in spite of being doubled by my OB—were not calming my anxiety. My skin was crawling and on fire, and my body was aching. The only thing I could get down was Ensure nutrition shakes, and I would force them down like medicine three times a day. I moved into the guest room full time, but it now felt like a tomb, an altar to the god of sleep that had abandoned me.

We'd gone into crisis mode. I was getting very irrational and had trouble completing sentences. Horribly, hours turned into days and no sleep ever came. By then, I was convinced I was dying, and was really just hanging on minute to minute. I remember in the middle of this, thinking I had to hold Tessa one last time in case I didn't survive another night. I lay on the couch with her on my body, and felt I was just clinging to life. Paul snapped a picture of me holding her that fills me with dread now when I see it. I was so desperate, and yet, in that photo, I'm just peacefully laying on the couch holding a baby.

The drug regime had become so complicated that I had to make up a chart to check off what I was taking when. My OB warned me that taking a lot of these at once would sedate me so completely as to stop my heart and kill me, which was starting to sound better and better. As the crisis escalated, and I was on my third day in a row without any sleep at all, she warned us both that I was on the verge of a total breakdown.

While my OB had us both on the phone, she told Paul that I might be having suicidal thoughts and that he needed to hide all the medications from that point on. When someone is that sleep-deprived they might make a quick, irreversible decision to just end it all to escape the pain. Then she made me promise that I wouldn't harm myself, and that I would tell her or someone else first if I was thinking anything like that.

How do you tell someone who loves you that you're thinking of ending your life because the carcass you're inhabiting is tortured and pained and doesn't work anymore? How can you be totally honest about how dark your soul has become, and how there is no indication that you're going to be free of it, ever?

I had those thoughts. But in the back of my brain there was some small memory of a piece of logic telling me that this would pass. That in spite of everything I was feeling, everything I believed to be true right now—that everything was hopeless, sucked dry of love or happiness or peace—despite every indicator that my life was now over, there was some little fragment of a sentence saying that this can happen and this can end. Maybe this was just postpartum depression, and maybe this was just chemical, and maybe if I could just ride it out, I'd survive.

I realized the only way out was to confess it all to Paul.

When I was done, he held me in his arms and started weeping. He told me how much he loved me, how much he needed me, how devastated he would be if I died. It was my thread back to life; he was the only thing that could penetrate the black loneliness of the hell I was in. His body next to mine holding me, rocking me, was my only hope. In his arms, I could feel that silver thread of love—of life, really—that I had felt the first time he'd ever held me. Paul took over on the drug regime, hiding the bottles from me to make sure I took no more, and no less, than what the doctor had dictated.

That night, I begged him for a dose of Nyquil on top of the other drugs to try and knock me out and break the cycle. He relented, and I hoped to be knocked over by a drug combo sledge-hammer. When my eyes popped open sometime later, my heart was pounding, and I prayed that many hours had gone by. To my shock and horror, it was a pathetic twenty minutes that had passed. It wasn't working. Nothing was working. I was in a tail-spin now.

Another twenty-four hours came and went with no relief. I got out of bed and into the bathtub, my only sanctuary. I lay in a couple inches of water and watched the trickle from the fau-cet roll down my foot and leg, feeling the anxiety noose pulling tighter around my neck. Paul came in the bathroom and said he needed to go out. He looked panicked and distraught, which was so unlike him. He said he was going to leave me alone for a couple hours to see his kids over at his ex-wife's house. I looked up into his face from miles away on the bottom of the bathtub, and told him, "I can promise you I will not do anything when you're gone. And I could even promise you that I won't do any-thing tonight. But you need to do something. I don't care what it is, but you need to do it."

After he left, I crawled back into my tomb of a room. I took all the medications he'd left me for that evening's dose and got back in that torture chamber called a bed and lay there in the darkness just rocking myself, the dry scratch of the humidifier blasting away, the burn in my legs and arms driving me to distraction, and sleep just out of my grasp. Tessa seemed a million light-years away at the far end of the house with the night nurse. I'd held her earlier that day and was terrified to realize that for the first time I felt nothing for her. She was like some doll I just wanted to give back now.

Around 2:00 a.m., when day had turned into deep night again, the boundaries between them long lost, I desperately reasoned it wouldn't hurt to add some Unisom to the mix; perhaps it would be just the right thing to tip me over the cliff and into sleep. I tiptoed into the master bedroom and was startled when Paul bolted upright. "Jessie, it's time," he said. "We have to go to the hospital." He had made a decision; it had to stop.

Earlier that evening, Paul had actually gone to consult with a good friend who was well versed in pharmacology. When Paul told him what had been going on, what drugs I was on, and the amounts, the lack of food, the lack of sleep, he had laid down the law. It was time to go to the hospital. It was that simple. Before leaving, with tears streaming down my face, I kissed Tessa's sweet hands and cheeks as she slept.

We drove to the emergency room at three in the morning, and twelve hours later, after being evaluated by many different doctors and nurses, I'd been checked into a room in the psych ward at Huntington Hospital. There was a bolt of terror running through me as I was wheeled into the building. I was putting myself in the hands of strangers who may or may not know what the hell they were doing. I kept asking Paul if this was the right thing to do. The pain on his face, the worry and the fear that he was trying to suppress were heartbreaking, and really the only answer I needed.

A nurse took me to my room, and I was horrified to see that I would not be alone. I'd be sharing with someone, who was suddenly up in my face, grinning and shaking my hand, welcoming me to her room. I looked around and wanted to leave instantly. There were two small, hard single beds, a single window, huge fluorescent lights overhead, and nothing else. The nurse informed me that there would be checks every half hour throughout the day and, insanely, throughout the night too. That would mean someone coming into the room via the heavy hospital door with its industrial latch and shining a flashlight in my face to make sure I was still alive.

The patients, both men and women, who suffered from extreme anxiety were pacing up and down the hall and talking to whoever would listen to their stream of personal hell; my roommate was an elderly woman who talked incessantly. The check-in to the ward was a one-on-one meeting that was conducted by a woman so loud and incompetent that I had to go get Paul just to have a witness to the kind of care that he was leaving me in. My panic was at full tilt by now. They'd taken all my clothes and locked away anything with more than a three-foot cord, belt, or ribbon for fear of patients attempting to hang themselves. There was no way that I was going to stay here. No way.

By now I was, really and truly, a crazy person. All I wanted was a quiet room and a horse-sized, hospital-issued pill that would knock me off my feet. And it looked like none of that was going to happen: we found out the psychiatrist who would be able to prescribe me the drugs I needed had gone for the day. This was the breaking point for Paul. He leapt out of his chair and practically climbed over the counter to grab the head nurse who dispensed the drugs.

Turns out the doctor had previewed my chart before he left and had prescribed some drugs for that night, with plans to meet with me the next day. Still, I didn't think I should stay at this nuthouse and was telling Paul so. Clearly, this had been a huge mistake and we had to go home. I was so afraid I was shaking. God bless him, he came and knelt before me and begged me, with tears in his eyes, to please, please, please stay and give it a try. He didn't know what else to do and this was his last resort. Would I please stay for him, and for Tessa? Looking into that strong face that I loved so much, and seeing the pain he was in was more than I could bear. So I agreed to stay. I watched him walk down the hall and out the door, which locked behind him.

There was something freeing about being at the very bottom of the barrel. My biggest fear had been realized. I stood there in my hospital socks and robe, wrapped up in the emergency room blanket, my life smashed on the floor. It was easy to resign myself to it on some level; I didn't have to fight anymore. I was in a hospital. It was their job to take care of me and make me better. I didn't have to make any more decisions. I didn't have to continue crashing from drug to drug, schedule to schedule, like I had been doing for weeks. I didn't have to do anything except heal myself.

I went to get the drugs that I had been on and found that the new doctor had taken me off everything. There was a standing prescription for Klonopin that was accessible to me every four hours as needed, and some huge, old school sleeping pill waiting for me for that night.

As I unpacked my meager belongings, I could see that I was already starting to feel differently. It was like when you've been on a long flight, and by the time you're a few hours in, you're so tired you think you could fall asleep standing up. But just before the plane lands, you have a burst of energy. My own personal flight had been going on for seven weeks, and I finally had the feeling that we were landing soon.

I called Paul at bedtime because I knew that he was in his own agony over what was happening and the choice he'd had to make, and I just wanted him to know that I felt the first tiny bit of relief. I could hear him fighting tears on the other end of the line. As I put down the phone, I felt such gratitude for him, for all he'd done, for all the love he'd shown, for the courage to take me to the hospital, to fight to make me stay.

This amazing man was so new to my life, and yet was part of the biggest things that had ever happened to me—falling in love, moving in together, getting pregnant, going through that difficult nine months, blending our lives and our families, eloping, and then giving birth to our daughter—and now all this. It's amazing to me that someone can explode into your life so intensely, so suddenly, and so late in the game.

Soon my roommate came in and went to bed. Within minutes she was asleep, and seconds after that I heard snoring so loud that it shook the room. All the calm that had started building since giving over to this hospital experience suddenly collapsed. There was no way I would be able to sleep through this, and honestly, I never thought I could sleep through the bed checks either. I went into the hall to the nurses' station. The night nurse asked why I wasn't in bed, and I told him the situation. He let me know that there were no other rooms or beds available in the whole ward. The place was packed. Panicking, I realized I'd have to call Paul to come get me after all.

And then another nurse said these magic words: "Well, there is the Quiet Room."

I don't know if I can describe the glory and hope that those words put in my heart. It turns out they had a room, so nicely named, for patients when they flip out. They could take them in there and tie them down until reinforcements came. It had no windows, and only one door that locked from the outside with a reinforced observation window. The only thing in the room was a platform with a vinyl pad on top, bolted to the floor with metal rings all around the edge for the restraints. It sounded like heaven to me.

Another huge perk to this weird and wonderful room was that because of the observation window, the security checks could be done throughout the night without opening the door. I begged them to let me go to the Quiet Room, explaining my desperate-for-sleep circumstances, and after sideways glances at each other, they agreed that I could, though if a patient got agitated in the night, they'd have to kick me out. I ran to my room, grabbed all my bedding, and dragged it into my new quarters.

I was almost cheery as I got my final dose of medication for the night, then climbed on the table/bed with a book, hoping against all hope for that wave of sleepiness that had eluded me for so long. Sure enough, in a few glorious minutes, it arrived: that heavenly feeling of droopy eyes and drugged, peaceful waves of sleep.

The next thing I knew it was 4:00 a.m. and I had to pee. I was in shock. I'd slept for five hours straight. I got up to go to the bathroom, and when I got back, I felt like I might actually be able to fall asleep again. And Lord have mercy on my soul, I did. Some time around 8:30 a.m., the nurses knocked on the door to wake me up. That one night of sleep broke the panic cycle, and by the end of that new day, I was almost completely myself again. The crazy, moaning, terrified, desperate zombie I'd been the week before was gone, and I was back. I was still shaky and scared that the insomnia could descend on me again at any time, but I was profoundly, miraculously myself again.

I learned a lot that day about what had gone wrong. The psychiatrist on call came to visit with me and we discussed the medicines I'd been taking, as instructed by my OB. As I listed them one by one, and their amounts, I could see shock on his face. Finally, he said, "Whoa, that's a lot of Benzos," a phrase I would hear a few times as people reviewed my medical history that week. It seemed I was having an adverse reaction to them, causing much of the burning ache in my limbs and pounding of my heart that had been torturing me.

The great news was that I was bouncing back quickly. The twelve-hour check-in process I'd endured in the E.R. probably saw me through the beginning of the withdrawal process, so that by bedtime that night the new medication could do its job. I was still rattled and having anxiety attacks, but nothing compared to where I'd been.

Soon, it was time to start group therapy. During the first session, I looked around the room at the ragged bunch of us. The other patients could have no idea that I'd had a bold life before all this. To them I was just another haggard crazy person who had washed up onto their shore. Who knew what stories the other people in this room could tell? One woman started talking about her imminent departure from the hospital because her medical benefits had run out, but she didn't know if she could cope. Her life on the outside sounded horrible, and she was being tossed back into it, still a desperate mess. She was struggling to get her head right, just like I was. I realized the best way to help her might be by telling my story, and that through my struggle, she might find comfort.

I talked about failing so terribly, feeling so ashamed and lost. And now, here I was at the bottom rung of the ladder, checked into a hospital with a newborn at home, with everyone but me taking care of her. Right then in that session, I let go of it. A kindness toward myself flooded in. I thought, *You can just stay here for a while and rest. It's going to be okay.* I opened my eyes and there were tears running down the faces of a few other people in the circle. It was a relief for all of us to just acknowledge where we were and how it felt, and to take a moment of rest.

The stories that I heard over the next two days were simply heartbreaking. Many of the patients had tragic childhoods, filled with fear and pain and loss. One woman spoke of witnessing her mother's violent suicide as a young girl. One sweet older man was so deeply sunk in his depression his head would just curl down on his body and he would shut off. I found myself getting more and more drawn into their life stories, their hearts. I wanted to help, and found little ways that I could, maybe in a way that the staff couldn't simply because they weren't sitting where we were. I understood the emotional mental loops these people were in; I understood how these treacherous waves of anxiety could rise out of nowhere and drown you. And in trying to help, I felt more and more like my old self.

However, I was worried that there were no other women with postpartum depression and that I was not going to get the help I needed here. I finally had a session with the head social worker there and told her my fears. This woman was wonderful. She told me that what she had seen over the years was that the source of the anxiety didn't really matter in the end. The battle was with the anxiety itself, not with the problem the anxiety had attached to. She closed our meeting by asking me if she could take me through a guided meditation. She had me blow up an imaginary red balloon and said that with each breath in, I was taking in healing air, and with each breath out, I was filling the balloon with every worry and anxiety I had. In and out, in and out. My mind was racing around gathering all the worries I had, all the fears that I couldn't do it or wasn't good enough or was doing it wrong, all the anxiety about being broken and unable to sleep, all the uncertainty around my life with its new baby, new husband, new town, new stepkids, new everything. I just blew and blew all those things into that balloon, scouring every corner of my brain for the seeds of fear and doubt that had taken hold there until I couldn't think of anything I'd left out. Then it slowly floated away and I watched it drift off into the sky, getting smaller and smaller and smaller until I could see it no more.

Afterward, I felt dramatically changed. I realized that I hadn't been feeling anything but panic for weeks because I'd been so locked up with the anxiety. I knew in my core when that meditation was over that I was really going to be okay. I walked out of that room a free woman.

Visiting hours were later that afternoon, and I couldn't wait to see Tessa and Paul, who came as soon as they could. He walked down the hall with her in her carrier and I could see the shock on his face. He knew instantly that I was back. He took me in his arms and we held each other for a long time. Then I took Tessa out of the carrier and wrapped myself around her, drinking in her scent, her skin, her loveliness. It hurt my heart to see how scared Paul was, how afraid he was that it would suddenly come back. But somehow, I just knew it wouldn't. The bad drugs were out of my system, my body wasn't in torture anymore, I'd been able to sleep, and mostly, I felt like myself again. The fever had broken.

My hospital stay lasted three nights and may have saved my life.

Six months later, we had our "real" wedding. It ended up being a spectacular event. Paul and I had been through so much together, and now it was time to celebrate this enormous moment in our lives. I wanted to celebrate my love for Paul and all he'd become to me, and celebrate the joy of becoming a mother to my baby girl. Nothing I have done or been through will ever compare to the wonder that Tessa has brought into my life, and it has left me forever altered for the better. In my heart, I wished for this to be just the beginning of our love, our family, our experience, our story. I wished for it all to grow into whatever magical thing it wanted to be.

And, extraordinarily, that's exactly what has happened. I had been released from the floods of the anxiety from postpartum depression and stopped trying and fighting so hard to push it away. It was Paul who held me tight when I had broken apart and his deep love for me showed me how to love myself when I needed it most. Our marriage had been forged by fire and I felt

we could survive anything. It was all a gift, in the end, for it was
in those darkest hours that I found the greatest treasure.

> *Note to self:*
>
> **When you are most afraid
> to tell the truth, it is absolutely vital
> that you do.**

A Love to Remember

GISELLE FERNANDEZ

Giselle Fernandez is a five-time Emmy Award–winning journalist and president of F Squared Enterprises, which concentrates on Latin-themed television and film productions, corporate and personal branding and marketing, and philanthropic ventures worldwide. She currently resides in California with her husband, John, and four-year-old daughter, Talei.

As I slide slowly into my fiftieth year, a time of deep searching and soulful contemplation of what's been and yet to be, I find myself obsessed with the excavation of what truly makes life meaningful, successful, and wildly worth the adventure. When you reach what you hope to be the halfway mark of life, you feel the frantic hands of Mother Time all over you. Something in you springs straight up from a dead sleep wanting to seize purpose, power, and reason for being as never before. All your dreams, did you live them, and is there still time? The thrust forward is thwarted by slamming on our own brakes, as if your insides know there's no going forward in a mad dash before retracing the years that have led you to who you are today.

My God, how you do look back. You watch your life as if you're watching someone else's movie, often surprised by the twists and turns, as if you had no hands on the wheel. You crawl into the cave with a searchlight retracing the story of you that's unfolded by chance or design, the gems that adorn and crown your life, the choices you made that define you. And of course, along this sentimental journey, there is no escaping those you've loved, especially if they have never left you; especially if it's a love that shaped your future and the very essence of your being.

I had such a love.

It's here I so easily surrender to the memories. I'm slung back joyously almost twenty-five years to a young and vibrant me, full of life and hungry for every moment. I can see and feel that me in my mind's eye as if it were all happening now. I was just starting out in my career, filled with big dreams, ideas, and ambitions, and very much of the belief that there was one love in the world tailor-made especially for me.

God, how I love rewinding the years to relive the moment we first met. It was magical. I was living in Los Angeles, anchoring the news for a local television station, and I was being recruited by news directors all over the country. I was hot and in demand and the world was my oyster; I had a hunger and drive to succeed and not a single doubt that I wouldn't. How I wish I could have kept that spirit. I'd been wined and dined in New York, Miami, and L.A. by well-coiffed news directors and station managers, put up in fine hotels and taken to lavish meals. I had offers in all three markets. I remember feeling on top of the world. My agent said there was interest in Chicago at the CBS station as well, but I wasn't interested. New York, with the number one station in the country, was where I was going. "If I can make it here/I'll make it anywhere," so that is exactly where I had my sights set. It was only at the insistence of my agent that I took the Chicago interview, for bargaining power with the other stations. I did not want to go.

I flew to the Windy City, planning to leave as quickly as I had arrived, and reluctantly waited to interview with the news director. I'd read up on him as I did them all, and he certainly had a history and lore worth reading about. Ron Kershaw was known as a maverick, a hard-partying, renegade newsman who networks put up with despite his unorthodoxy simply because he turned third place stations into first place stations in record speed. He was known for his take-no-prisoners, no-nonsense knack for taking on the establishment and telling stories that matter, that expose corruption and protect the common man. He was also known for having been the boyfriend of the late famous newswoman Jessica Savitch, with whom he'd had a volatile relationship. They had broken up already when her car crashed into a river in upstate New York on October 23, 1983, but her death was said to have destroyed him. I was told that the movie *Up Close and Personal* was about their love affair.

Kershaw certainly had a different résumé than the customary suit-clad news directors I had already met with, and clearly a different dress code. I was sitting in the WBBM lobby waiting when a robust man in his early forties shuffled down the hall wearing loafers, no socks, a Chicago Bears sweatshirt, jeans, and a baseball cap. He was holding a cup of coffee in one hand and a lit cigarette in the other. This was not your typical suit, and he charmed me at hello.

The first words out of his mouth were, "Hello, Princess."

Princess?

"Yeah," he said. "You're a princess."

I was so taken off guard by his whole commanding rebel presence, I just smiled awkwardly, knowing right away this would be no normal encounter. He was exciting, and I was on alert and sensing the need to step up my game in order to keep up.

As I look back, I realize I was the girl who had wished all her life she had the kind of doting daddy who would call her "Princess." Instead, some quirky guy in a baseball cap and loafers, with a trace of a Southern drawl from the hillbilly Blue Ridge Mountains of South Carolina, uttered those precious words. And at twentysomething, they rang through me and somehow managed to sound all my bells and whistles.

I walked through that newsroom nervously, knowing I was walking through the halls where legendary reporters dug away at their stories—reporters like Bulldog Drummond, who covered the Mob, and Mike Flannery, who covered Chicago politics. Chicago's CBS was home to the first Kennedy/Nixon debates. It was a no-joke, gritty newsroom, and especially so while under the reign of this legendary and notorious newsman. I was in complete awe. I wasn't thinking about New York just then. All I could think was that I had made it, and I could barely contain myself.

I followed Ron into his large offices, where portraits of Robert E. Lee and Stonewall Jackson stared proudly from his walls, among the other more colloquial memorabilia that painted a portrait of the man behind the desk: lots of sports stuff, news headlines and awards for stations he'd turned around with kick-ass stories he'd had the guts to put on the air. There was a lot of rock-'n'-roll memorabilia, too. U2's "I Still Haven't Found What I'm Looking For" was playing on his stereo as I walked in.

Ron threw his feet up on his desk and immediately leaned back in his chair, informing me that he knew of all my offers in the other cities. He told me that was just dandy, but if I wanted to be a real reporter and make a damn difference, and not just be a television star, I'd make the right choice and come work for him in Chicago.

No words were wasted. He spent a bit of time talking about this work being a mission to expose ivory tower corruption in order to protect the common man. He talked about the importance of telling a story that matters and having the balls to challenge the powers that be.

"The people have a right to know," he said. "That's what we do. That's America. Want to be a part of what makes America great, Princess? Then come to Chicago. You want to be a star? You got your offers."

That was it. He smiled his wry smile with that mischievous gleam in his eyes and told me to go out and look around, take it all in, and he'd see me at dinner with his Kentucky-bred sidekick, the assistant news director, after the six o'clock news.

I was floored. God, was I floored. Somehow, he'd spoken to my soul. I wanted desperately to be real and authentic; I wanted to be the best reporter in the world and not just a pretty reader of news. He tapped into the idealism of my youth—into the dream of making a difference, of going after authority to uphold the voice and dreams of the common man. He was the rebel *with* a cause, and I—was wide-eyed and blown away by the whole scene.

I left his office with Robert E. Lee staring down at me, and I was ready to go to battle. *This isn't just a job*, I remember thinking. *It is my destiny.*

After the six o'clock newscast was over, I piled into Ron's Nissan Sentra with his news director, but instead of taking me to a nice restaurant for a professional dinner—as the other networks had done—Ron took us to a burger joint, where he told great tales of Jessica Savitch and the rough-and-tumble times he had getting the tough stories when he was on the air. He then took us to a blues bar, where we all drank more than we should have. This was all capped off with a renegade ride in his car along the lakefront, the three of us drunk and singing along to the songs on the radio as if we'd known each other for years.

It had been one of the best days of my life, and I prayed the whole ride back to the hotel that I wouldn't throw up from all the drinking. I promised God I would never swear again, never drink, never think bad thoughts if He just let me get back to the hotel without vomiting and humiliating myself.

We pulled up to the Ritz-Carlton, where the network was putting me up. When the valet opened the door, Kershaw didn't even bother turning from the wheel. He simply asked, "So, Princess, you coming to Chicago?" And with no hesitation I said, "Yes I am, sir." "Attagirl," he said, as I stumbled out of the car.

Later, as I threw myself on that gorgeous white duvet and nestled into the downy pillows, the likes of which I'd never felt before, I immediately called my best friend in Phoenix and told her I'd just fallen in love with the man I was going to marry. I remember her saying, "If he's going to be your boss, that's probably not a good idea."

When I returned home to Los Angeles, my agent was totally

surprised to learn I'd committed to Chicago. The station I was working for refused to let me out of my contract, so I had to wait nine months to make the move, but Ron was willing to wait. In the meantime, he was all I could think about. He made me want to be a better reporter.

A couple of months after I'd returned to L.A., Ron called to say he was coming into town for a news directors' conference and would like to see me. I was both excited and nervous. He came to the studio while we were live on the air, put his feet up on a table, and lit a cigarette. "You can't smoke in the studio," the stage manager told him, but he didn't seem to care. I wondered if he knew I was crazy about him.

He'd brought me crystallized violets and said they were good luck, and he showed me a little bag of gems that he wore on a leather strap around his neck, also for good luck. He was a mystical man, and I couldn't help feeling magic in his presence.

That night, he drove me to his hotel in Westwood, where a couple of friends he knew in the business were meeting him for drinks. We met up with his friends, and we spent the night drinking and talking about the news and all the great stories they'd covered. Once again, I was struck by how much Ron loved the business, and he infused in me that sense of mission and responsibility to the people of this country, who have a right to know the truth about the world they're living in. He was big on exposing consumer fraud, police abuse, and health care exploitation. He was wild for stories that showed the workingman being ripped off, and was keen on taking down political and industry leaders and systems that exploited the poor and powerless for their own profit and gain. He also loved a great sports story, whether it was about the thrill of victory or the devastation of defeat. He was all about those Bears and Cubs, and clearly loved Chicago's pride in their sports teams. And, of course, there was rock 'n' roll. He loved music, and wherever he was, it played loud and strong.

By about three in the morning, his friends were making out in the corner of the room; a new round of drinks had just arrived, and I knew it was time to leave. It felt like ripping a clam out of its shell, but I stood up and bid Ron goodnight anyway.

As I walked toward the door, he said, "Princess, you sure you want to leave?" I can still feel the breath and the sigh that swallowed me as I turned around and said, "Yep, it's time." He said, "If you go, go because you don't want to stay. But don't go because you think it's the right thing to do."

I told him he was going to be my boss, so it was probably not a good idea to stay, and then I started the walk down that long hallway toward the elevators. When I looked back, he was leaning on the inside of the door.

"Don't you at least want to kiss me goodbye?" he asked, but I just kept walking toward that elevator, telling myself to keep going. When I pressed the button, he called out, "You'll regret this one day."

By the time those doors closed, I already did. But I had no idea how much I'd regret losing that kiss and that night until years later. Even now, a quarter century gone by, I wish I'd had the presence and courage to stay. I should have kissed him passionately. Because he was right: I left not because I wanted to, but because it was what I thought I was supposed to do.

When I finally arrived in Chicago and moved into my high-rise flat near the Loop, I was both excited and scared out of my wits. The newsroom was so much bigger and more sophisticated than I had remembered it, and I was clearly perceived as a pretty reader walking in the door in a new age of journalism that was corrupting the rugged and real tenets of the business. Making matters worse, Kershaw was away on business and wouldn't be back for weeks, which was so disappointing. I was finally there, and he wasn't. Though he had left a bag of crystallized violets on my desk, which made me smile.

The assistant news director picked up the slack for Kershaw and gave me some guidance, but it was clear she was questioning where my bravado had gone upon my arrival. It was tough getting my sea legs, and Chicago is not the kind of town to coddle a newcomer; nor was that particular newsroom in any hurry to make me feel welcome. I was pretty much on my own, and even when Kershaw finally returned, it was not as I'd imagined.

He seemed indifferent to me, and I remember just trying to keep my emotions and expectations in check. This was my new job, and I had to concentrate on it and nothing else. In the morning meetings, he'd go over every story, and when it was my turn, he was always extra tough. "Congratulations, Princess. In one story, you tried, convicted, and hanged the guy. All in a minute thirty." It was like a dagger in my heart, stabbed into me in front of everyone. He was pushing me to be better, I knew, teaching me at every turn. He had no patience for fools or failure. I thought he was cruel at times, but looking back, I know it wasn't that. He was just trying to make me a better journalist.

I cried a lot in the bathroom those first days on the job, and I hated him for a while after that. There was no special treatment. There was no sense whatsoever of the chemistry or magic I'd felt between us. He was hard-core and all business until after the newscasts. Then, he would take the whole crew and news team across the street to the Gold Star, a cool blues joint where everyone would drink and relax. Most times I didn't go, and when I did, I left after one drink. While there, I would watch him hold court with his team, still in awe of him in spite of myself. He had this amazing way of drawing everyone to him. People wanted his attention, his imprimatur. He lifted everyone's game. He gave you the feeling that wherever he was, that was the place to be. When I'd get up to leave, I always felt his stare. "Leaving so soon, Princess?" he'd ask, and I'd nod, telling him I had to work tomorrow, slinking out with a smile, convincing myself that I'd dodged a bullet.

Then came the floods. There was horrible rain that caused massive flooding in Chicago, and O'Hare Airport was completely engulfed in water. No one could get in or out unless they waded through a waist-deep lake. I tried to get out of a live shot there that Kershaw assigned to me, explaining to him that I just wasn't ready yet, but he told me to get out of his office and get to the airport. I was petrified. I didn't want to fail, and I certainly didn't want to fail in front of him.

After twelve hours of live coverage, I was hanging back in the live truck, completely exhausted and still dressed in rubber flood pants, when a call came in. The crew told me it was Kershaw, who never calls. I picked up the phone, and all he said was, "Princess, you're a fucking star." Then he hung up.

I fell back in my chair, closed my eyes, smiled the biggest smile from the inside out, then let out a "Whoooo hooooo!" as loud as a bullhorn. It was one of the greatest moments of my life.

That night I did go to the Gold Star, and I partied with the team, feeling like I belonged to the greatest club in the world.

We had kicked butt on the story, and Kershaw was elated. The team was tired, but feeling good about the coverage. Kershaw knew how to get the best out of everyone, and how to make you feel part of his team if you carried your weight. I'd never have another news director—or boss, for that matter—like him again. That night, as I got up to go, he grabbed my hand and said, "Stay a while." It was the first time since I'd come to Chicago that I saw that look in his eye, and I didn't want to go. This time, I stayed.

I went home with him that night, and for the next month we had the most magical, crazy, wildly in love moments I'd ever experienced. I worked the night shift, so I would see him during the day and the weekends, and we tried our best to hide our relationship at work, though it wasn't easy. Eventually, we decided we had to tell management we were in love. I knew it would be tragic for me if the team found out; a relationship with the news director was dangerous. But I was so in love and so taken with this bigger-than-life man who had rocked every inch of my world. It wasn't an easy decision after all the hard work I'd put into making a name for myself at the network, but I told Ron I would be the one to leave and work somewhere else. For me, loving him was worth the sacrifice.

But before we had a chance to tell anyone, Ron became terribly ill.

I was leaving for work one morning, and he remained in bed, not feeling well. I told him I would call later to check on him, but by the time I did, he was already in the hospital. In a matter of days, he was diagnosed with pancreatic and liver cancer, which had already spread throughout his body. And just like that, he was given only two months to live.

I was at the hospital with Ron's son when the doctors broke the news. Ron's son screamed and fell to his knees sobbing. I could barely face Ron myself. When I did, I just held him in my arms. All he could say was, "Why now, when I've finally found you?"

People from all over the news business flocked to the hospital to see him, people whose careers he'd started and given rise to. Our colleagues from the newsroom came too, and it soon became clear that my role there was not just as his employee. I didn't care. I was too stricken with grief.

Besides, it didn't matter what everyone else thought. It was Ron who drew me near and asked that I stay closer than ever. When you are called to service of the soul and rise to that calling, there is no greater gift in the world.

Over the next nine months, Ron went into work less and less. I cared for him at home around the clock, leaving only to continue my shifts as a reporter in a newsroom that quickly turned vitriolic. Ron and I flew to Canada for alternative treatments and drove to Vermont so he could see the snow. He wanted to see Rhode Island again and his favorite place, Castle on the Hill in Newport, where he'd spent time with Jessica. I did all that he wished, while watching him whittle down from one hundred eighty pounds to just eighty.

Still, while he may have lost weight and weakened, he never lost his courage or his humor or his convictions. I've never seen such bravery. When he took his final breaths as he died in my arms, his last words were, "I love you so much." I can still hear him say it. It's engraved in me forever.

A light went out of me that day. I felt completely hollowed out, lonely and grieving for the kind of magic I knew would not come around again. It seemed to me then that I would never get over the pain. Looking back at that moment in time, I marvel now at my strength and capacity to love at such a young age. I'm more proud of that than anything else I've ever done in my life.

Ron was just forty-three years old, so young and so brilliant, with so much left to do. My God, he was such a big soul! And though he's been gone now for so long, he's still alive to me. I still feel the power of his smile and his humor and his passion. He would have hated to see what has become of the news business. I often think of him, and what he'd advise on a story. He would have been so fired up through the Bush years, through Bernie Madoff and the Wall Street collapse, the mortgage crisis that thrust this country into recession. Through it all, he would have been championing the call of the working class. And boy, would he have had a lot to say about moose-hunting Sarah Palin!

As for me, I did go on to love again. Eventually, I got married and had a beautiful child, a wonderful family. And I had so many adventures in the news business. It's true that time heals all, but what's also true is the immense power of love—the enduring imprint of someone else on the person you become and the way you live your days. *That* doesn't die. It shapes you forever.

Today, at nearly fifty, I would never walk away from a kiss I really wanted. Not ever again. I still love violets and U2, and I keep the bag of gems Ron wore around his neck in my treasure box. I love the me that endured that journey and still cherishes those moments. I would live them all over again, even in spite of the pain, just to have been loved by someone like Ron. He was one of the most blessed adventures of my life. I loved and lost, and now I mark those experiences among the most defining of my being. To remember Ron is to remember what I'm capable of, and my God, how it awakens that passion for truth. That I'll take with me into every new chapter of my life.

Note to self:

There is no adventure
greater than love.

The Man Who Fell from the Sky

STEPHANIE FORBERG

Stephanie Forberg is an art teacher who lives and works outside Boston, Massachusetts. She has four healthy parents, two teenaged sons, and two dumb cats.

In the summer of 2005 I made a pretty significant resolution: I decided to remain single for the rest of my life. I was forty-five years old, the mother of two boys, gainfully employed, in good health, with a loving family and abundant friends—and absolutely sick to death of the dating wars and the fruitless, frustrating, and probably hopeless search for True Love.

I was living outside Chicago at the time and had been happily divorced for more than four years. An extended serious relationship had been followed by eighteen months of fun and games on Match.com; I dated quite a few men I men on that site, became infatuated once or twice, dumped and got dumped, received one marriage proposal, and generally sowed all the wild oats I'd kept so safely tucked away in my youth.

By the spring of 2005, however, being a player was beginning to get old. Glamorous as it had been, it really wasn't "me."

I wanted what so many single people do: love, passion, a life-long soul mate! Or, failing that, at least a halfway decent man who would consider commitment and whose company I could amicably tolerate, if not actively enjoy. But it wasn't happening. When the latest relationship (in which I had invested an unwarranted amount of hope and energy) faltered, I decided I was done with the whole dating scene altogether. I resigned myself to the idea that there were many wonderful things in my life but apparently a fulfilling relationship was not going to be one of them. *Well, fine,* I told myself. I would enjoy all those blessings to the fullest, revel in the advantages of solitude and independence, and try hard not to dwell on the drawbacks. In the back of my mind something my mother had said when I was a child still lingered—"I think you'll be lucky in love." I'd taken this comment as deeply to heart as a personal note from Nostradamus, but it seemed my mother was going to be wrong on this point. Sometimes mothers are wrong, after all.

In early July, my boys and I settled into a little rental cottage on the coast of Cape Cod, Massachusetts, where I've spent every summer of my life. After a somewhat dissatisfying spring, I'd been looking forward to a delightful three-week vacation on the beach with my boys. One gray and windy Friday I drove them to their morning camp session, and then headed toward home for a few hours of chores. But as I drove by a road that ran out to the ocean, I impulsively turned down it. It didn't lead to our regular beach, and as the day was far too cold and dreary for sunbathing, I thought I'd just take a brisk walk by the water to enjoy the wind and the surf before addressing my to-do list.

I parked in the nearly deserted lot and walked to the top of the dune. Just then, like some silent, colorful, prehistoric pterodactyl, a paraglider floated into view and soared twenty feet directly over my head. Although I'd heard of these long, rectangular nylon parachutes, I'd never actually seen one before. I was startled and delighted by the sight and couldn't resist waving and calling out, "Looks like fun!" A disembodied voice from the black-helmeted figure in the harness dangling below the chute called back, "It is!"

I ran down the dune and began my walk along the shore, glancing up now and then to watch the figure of the paraglider drift beyond me down the dune line, then turn and glide in the opposite direction. Once when it passed overhead I raised my arms and playfully jumped in the air. "Come on up!" called the voice. "I wish I could!" I answered. It circled around a few more times and finally soared back up the beach behind me.

I continued on my walk and noticed something lying on the sand by the water's edge just ahead. As I got closer, I realized to my utter amazement that it was a harbor seal. Seals are no rarity on this beach—almost any day you can see them lolling or fishing just offshore—but to find one sprawled out on the sand was absolutely unique. In my half a century of summers here this was the first time I had ever seen that. Was it an omen? Previously I would never have suspected pinnipeds of having any "portent potential," but nowadays an encounter with them always fills me with a warm tingle of something like gratitude.

After watching the seal yawn and flick her flippers for a few minutes it began to rain, so I turned and headed back to the parking lot. Ahead of me in the distance I saw the paraglider again, but now as I watched he slowly settled on the beach and the wing fluttered to the ground. I picked up my pace, hoping to catch the flyer before he left, as I was curious to see the contraption up close. As I walked, I instinctively shook my hair free of my ponytail. (Mind you, exactly one week before I had sworn off men for the rest of my natural life. Hope really does relentlessly spring eternal!)

As I got closer, I saw that the pilot was a tall, slim, muscular, and devastatingly handsome man. We greeted each other with warm hellos and I asked all the obligatory questions about paragliding: how it worked, how long he'd been flying, etc. He answered me cheerfully, with obvious intelligence and humor. He spoke in a delicious and indefinable accent—it sounded like a generous dose of Irish with sprinkles here and there of German and French (it turned out he was Swiss). I think it's probably fair to say that I fell head over heels in love with him at that very moment, but I didn't admit it to myself for another four whole days.

We exchanged names and I helped him carry the glider back up the dunes to the parking lot, and then gave him a lift a few miles up the road to the next beach where his car was parked. We sat there talking and laughing for about half an hour until his friend, another paraglider, came over to point out that the rain had stopped and it was flyable again. My new friend Eric merely said, "That's okay—I'm good," and continued his conversation with me. His friend looked nonplussed. (Months later I realized that for a paraglider to turn down any chance to fly, after having driven most of the morning to get to a site, was pretty extraordinary.) My chores were long forgotten, and we spent the next two hours talking and laughing.

Finally I had to leave to pick my children up at camp. We exchanged numbers and agreed that if he happened to be back in the area in the next few weeks—he lived two hours away, and had only come to paraglide by the dunes—he would give me a call. I waved goodbye and was pulling out of the parking lot when he flagged me down to ask if I knew of a place nearby where he and his friend could get lunch. My car window was rolled down and he put his hand on top of the door. As I gave him directions, I lightly rested my hand on his; it's a moment we both remember for the palpable physical electricity we felt. I drove down the highway to the camp with a three-mile smile plastered on my face. *What a lovely experience*, I thought, fully expecting never to see him again. But it had been an enchanting encounter and had reaffirmed my faith in a good world.

I was genuinely shocked when I got a text message from him later that day thanking me for the lunch recommendation. Of course I wrote back, and after exchanging a few more messages he called to say that he'd probably be coming out to the Cape again in a few days to paraglide. We agreed to meet up. The next Tuesday, Eric, my sons, and I checked out the marginal wind conditions at the beach. It didn't appear that paragliding was going to be possible so instead we spent the day showing Eric around the area. We visited the ponds, the town, and the harbor; he seemed in no hurry to leave, and my boys gravitated to this warm, open, easygoing person as much as I did. But despite the fact that we now seemed to be officially friends, I honestly didn't dream for a moment that anything more significant could develop between us. I assumed he was involved with someone (how could any man so attractive and charming not be?) and frankly thought, as women so often do, that he was somewhat out of my league. Besides, I was celibate now, right?

Come evening, I suggested we all go out to dinner. My sons demurred, opting to stay home instead (thank God!), and Eric and I headed to a shoreside restaurant for a quiet meal together. Neither of us wanted the evening to end, so we continued with dessert at another restaurant for a few more hours, then returned to the first restaurant for a very long nightcap, and finally ended up at the town's only "late night" spot for beer and a laughable game of pool. There was no place left to go after that except the star-filled beach, where we had our first kiss. And our second. And our ninety-ninth.

After that night we spent as much time together as possible in my remaining two weeks on the East Coast. When I had to return to Chicago we racked up quintuple-digit frequent flier miles between Illinois and Massachusetts, and within weeks it was clear to me that I had to relocate.

By the following summer, I had moved heaven and earth to be near him. Because my oldest son was about to start high school back in Illinois, it made sense for him to stay there with my ex-husband, with whom I'd always maintained a good relationship. Still, it wasn't easy for any of us and I couldn't have done it without the unflagging support of my parents who, among other things, helped me pay for the move. By the time I made it to Massachusetts I'd divided my family, suffered huge financial losses, taken an inferior job, and stuffed all my possessions into a cramped apartment. But I was finally close to Eric.

And it was all worth it. A thousand times over.

Years after our chance encounter on the beach we are still deeply in love, amazingly compatible, profoundly grateful for and delighted by each other on a daily basis, and committed for life. He is everything I ever envisioned in my dreamy childhood, or fantasized about in my star-struck adolescence, or longed for in my pragmatic adulthood. He is my dearest friend, my life partner, my soul mate—and my genuine one true love. And the very best part of all? I'm his, too.

So, what's the moral of this little story? Maybe that the immediate vicinity of any seal at rest should be thoroughly investigated. Or that fairy-tale True Love is indeed real, and every once in a while some of us are stunningly lucky enough to find it. But above all I think the most important thing to remember is: keep looking up.

Note to self:

The fate you think you've chosen for yourself can be unsealed.

Things That Are Possible

NANCY HIMMEL

Former global head of Entertainment Marketing for a sports-wear label, Nancy Himmel changed careers in 2007 to become a film and television writer. She currently resides in Los Angeles, where she uses her years of international travel and real-life experiences as inspiration for her work.

When I was a little girl, I thought my dream life was one hundred percent possible. The knight in shining armor, white picket fence, big career, extreme happiness, perfection-in-every-way was just there in my future. I think a lot of people are raised to believe this to be true. I was definitely raised to believe anything is possible, and as I got older, I continued to hold on to the hope it was. But sometimes life throws you curve balls, and it's those unexpected moments that change you, define you, and make you grow a bit quicker, and become a lot stronger, then you ever could have imagined.

This very thing happened to me on a sunny December day when I was in high school. I had slept quite late, which was not unusual for me. As an overachieving senior, my weekends were about recovery from each week before. The house was quiet since my family had gone to get breakfast, and I had just gotten up and begun washing some clothes when the phone rang. My hands filled with dirty socks, I let it keep ringing. I was busy; whoever was calling could wait. But, then, it started ringing again. Still busy, I continued to ignore it. A pause, and then the phone began ringing once more. At that point, something didn't feel right, so I washed my hands and went to check the messages.

Before I could listen, the phone rang yet again. This time, I answered. It was one of my friends, and she was crying. "I'm so sorry," she said. "I don't know what to say. I can't believe it." I asked her what she was talking about, and the phone went silent. What seemed like an eternity passed before she finally said, "Oh my God. You don't know." I held my breath. And then I heard the words that will forever ring in my ears. "Nan. The car. They couldn't save him. I'm so sorry. He's gone."

As I stood in the middle of the long, empty hallway that led to the kitchen, with the morning sun piercing in through a window to my right and the door to the icy gray bathroom to the left, I froze. Suddenly the only thing I could see was his face staring back at me from the empty white wall ahead. It was the sweetest image of him I had, the last time I saw him. His blond hair had flopped over his big blue eyes as he'd handed me a single flower. He was not typically a romantic, and he gave it to me with such sweet, shy, childish hesitation. I'm not typically a girl who needs to be given flowers, but I had loved it.

At the memory, my legs gave way under my heavy heart. I leaned back to prop myself up but couldn't, and with every inch I slid down the wall the color in my face faded. My hand, which had been clenched to the phone, released. My long white nightshirt crept up my back as I neared the floor, leaving my skin exposed to the rough Berber carpet, but I felt nothing at all. Then, a chill came over me, and my body started to shake. Knees tucked in, arms clasped, I began to rock back and forth as I had when I was a child and I'd wanted to drown out the world. I needed to drown out all that was around me; at that moment the pain felt so raw, so deep.

I'm not sure how long I stayed there or how long it took me to pick up the phone again, but, painfully aware that I was alone in the house, I eventually did. As though I was on automatic pilot, I dialed the number for my brother, who was away at college. My tears were now flowing hard and fast, and my sobs were so uncontrollable that when he answered the phone, he didn't know it was me. When I was finally able to get out what had happened, that the tall, gentle, good-natured boy I had been dating for six months had suddenly died the night before after losing control of his car, he simply sat in silence and let me cry. Just knowing he was on the other end was enough. He didn't need to say a word and he knew it.

While the next few days are somewhat of a blur, I'll never forget the feeling I had when I went to see his family the day before the funeral. And though I'm not yet a mother, I can't imagine there being anything more painful than a parent losing a child. Facing them and seeing their pain made the loss all the more real. When I got home, my father answered the door and gave me a giant hug, and he told me that something had arrived for me while I was gone. I walked into the kitchen and found a beautiful bouquet of red roses with a card perched at the top. They were from my brother, and there were only two words written on the card; once again, he knew exactly what I needed to hear: "Love, Doug."

As a teenager on your way to adulthood, your concerns in life are supposed to be about social development and things that may look and feel earth-shattering at the time, but are minor in retrospect. They're not supposed to be about real life and death situations. I was thrown into the deep end of the pool of difficult life experiences, and it took a long time for me to wrap my head around what had happened and move on, a long time to get back to being or at least feeling like myself again. I wish I could explain how my recovery came about, but to this day I'm still not sure. I guess you could chalk it up to time.

Months later, I went off to college. Being in a new environment was hard, but good for me at the same time. New people to meet, places to become acquainted with, and my classes kept me occupied. I drank and ate like a champion, put on some college pounds to prove it, and learned to look at life in a hopeful, happy way again, though my dating life suffered. I think if you go through losing someone you care about in such a sudden way, and especially at a young age, something inside you changes.

The idea of opening up my heart again was petrifying. But, as luck would have it, I met a boy Sophomore year who, as hard as I tried to push him away, wouldn't let me. For months he waited for me to agree to go out with him, and for months I waited for him to give up. But he never did. He was the most persistent person I had ever met. We ended up dating for a few years, but broke up after graduation when life took us in different directions. I will forever be grateful for his kindness and patience.

As unimaginable as it had been to think about allowing myself to be vulnerable again to anyone in college, I never could have predicted how terrifying dating in the real world could be. In high school, your life is somewhat contained and safe in that everyone more or less knows everyone else's story. College, too. The real world is a completely unpredictable arena. And let's face it, everyone is just trying to find their way, but some are a little more lost than others. For a time I seemed to attract every one of those lost souls, and after growing more and more frustrated by these unfulfilling relationships, I learned to distract myself through work.

I was driven; I was focused; I never stopped moving up the corporate ladder until one day I woke up and was somehow overseeing a division of an international corporation. My job had me traveling the world, and I should have been on top of it; but I wasn't. Something was missing, and when I thought about what it might be, the answer was simple: I was alone.

One afternoon my mom called and left me a message asking what part of the planet I was on. Was I in Germany? Was I in Boston? She had no clue. When I heard the voice mail I thought, how have I let myself get so disconnected? I sat back and took a hard look at my life. I analyzed where I was, where I wanted to be, what I wanted, and what, if anything, I had done wrong to end up there. I realized that to protect my heart I hid in work, and I had done such a good job of it I'd lost myself along the way. I was too old to hug my knees and rock back and forth to drown my loneliness out, so I excused my lack of a love life under the guise that I was just too busy. But who would ever choose to be too busy to love?

So, I quit it all. I quit my job, the above-speed-limit race in the wrong direction, and for the next year I just regrouped. By forcing myself to look inside and reflect without a safety net of distractions, I finally regained the hope that the knight, the picket fence, and the happiness are indeed still possible. And without feeling like I had to throw myself into whatever job would keep me the busiest or most preoccupied, I recognized what I truly wanted to be: a writer. In fact, as ironic as this may sound, I discovered that I'm a comedy writer. There is nothing that makes me happier than to make others laugh; to know what true pain is and be able to bring pure joy feels like a gift. I also realized that the characters in the script of my life are far more colorful than any I could make up, and it made me appreciate them even more.

My pursuit of love is, yet again, accompanied by childlike hope, but now mixed with adult confidence. My journey has been one of avoidance, recovery, and self-protection, but also of appreciation and growth. Today, not only do I understand the importance of making time for the people around me but I'm again allowing people in. Because, in the end, all we can hope for are the amazing people who fill our lives, inspire our stories, and the possibility of someone to share this with.

Note to self:

**If you believe in your heart
that anything is possible,
it is.**

Waiting for Adele

JENNIFER HOPPE-HOUSE

Jennifer Hoppe-House, a playwright from Texas, has written over a dozen feature scripts for major studios. She worked on the Emmy-nominated series *Nurse Jackie* in its first two seasons and is now writing for *Damages* with her writing partner Nancy Fichman. She lives with the love of her life in a clean house, blessed with a magical old fig tree out back. She enjoys coffee, perhaps a little too much.

I started thinking about my one true love when I was six, usually just before I went to sleep. I would clutch a stuffed giraffe I'd named after Jermaine Jackson and imagine life with another person—not just any person, but *my* person—the one I missed (we'd never met, but I knew we would), the one who would fit me like the other half of a broken plate. I didn't imagine a husband, really, just the feeling: the feeling of being with someone who loved talking to me, who would make me laugh to the point of suffocation; a best friend who would spend the night every night; who would hold my hand until an impression was left in my palm. I mean, I was six; it wasn't a complicated fantasy, but the feelings were primal. I wanted to be in love.

I realized later that the reason I didn't picture a husband was because I was gay. This discovery hit me like a bus the summer after I'd turned seventeen. My epochal awakening is recorded in a journal, in bubbly, eleventh-grade handwriting:

July 10, 1981

Last night was bizarre and perfect and not the least bit confusing. I saw Kate at The Landing. We went to a friend of hers apartment. In other words, I sort of went home with her. I stayed up all night. Homosexual, definitely.

So that was that.

All I had to do now was find my one true love. It wasn't Kate, though she did begin a cycle of serial (sometimes semi-) monogamy, false alarms, and near misses that lasted twenty-two years. Still, in or out of relationships, I always imagined that somewhere someone—*my* one—was looking for me.

When I was thirty-eight, I decided to write an online personal ad. I'd fling my desires into the universe; compose a mature-but-irreverent, highly targeted message in a bottle; see if my person, my fated fix was paying attention. The headline was "I'm Pretty and I Cook." After that, I got down to business:

I'm successful and bright, but I've failed and been stupid more than a few times. I have a fairly peaceful life (as peaceful as life can be in a mean and mendacious industry) and I feel lucky every day (and annoyed sometimes, and pissed, but lucky nonetheless). I'm a very good friend to a select number of people, I love to be in the kitchen all day (but rarely get to do it), I question why we're here and consider the answers at least once a week in therapy, and I have an aversion to those gross Carl's Jr. commercials. I'm a lot of fun, but I like my solitude. Communication is key, and I prefer to do that with girls who know how to talk, who think in full sentences, who have been through a few things, who have grown in and out of relationships, and who are complete without me or anyone else. In a partner, I'm looking for intelligence, femininity, strength, humor, and humility. In short, I'm looking for someone sort of like me, but whose differences are complementary (I don't work in the yard—I leave that to you), whose life and clothes are her own, and whose pain has manifested in compassion, not in bitterness. I want a grown-up. I love girls who have become women. I'm attracted to femininity (butch just isn't my thing), to ambition (but for passion's sake, not for money), to beauty (but that doesn't mean youth). I'm drawn to warmth and quick wit. I love to be dazzled, but that's a rare thing. And finally, importantly, I have to see a photo (I know what I like).

Over the next couple of months, I had a few dates *without* destiny: the Drunk Girl, the Inappropriate Girl, the Agoraphobic. And then, incredibly, after all my years of waiting, my one true love—who had been strolling along the cyberspace shore—stumbled upon me.

Her subject line was "I'm Pretty and I Eat." She said that she'd never had the incentive to answer a personal ad, but that she'd laughed aloud at my profile and felt strangely compelled. She was a dietitian who specialized in treating individuals with HIV and AIDS. She said that she was close to her family, "committed to living consciously, warm, compassionate and reliable." She then added, "I like to crochet (the grandma in me!)" and attached two photographs. The first was of her with her mother (her mother!). The other, the money shot, was taken while she was on a medical mercy mission in Jamaica. She wore mint-colored scrubs and had just blown a blizzard of bubbles for a crowd of Jamaican children, whose hands were raised in an effort to seize the evanescence. Her skin was tanned, her eyes were warm, bright pools, and her hair was tied back, fully exposing a beatific smile; an astonishing smile; something that still brings me to my knees at least twice a day.

My one true love's name was Adele.

When I heard her voice on the phone, I knew I was in love. I don't mean the tone of her voice or the way she used language, although I was wild about those qualities, too—I mean its current, its flow, the way it carried me. That sounds insane, I know, but I was at home in her riptide; I was gone.

Twenty minutes into our first date, as she was doubled over with laughter about a painful yet hilarious childhood memory I'd shared, I had the reckless confidence to pronounce, "Well, it's clear we're going to be together for a while."

"Yep," she said, not even blinking.

And that was that.

Six years later, the California Supreme Court gave us a window to get married, and we did, on a balcony overlooking the Coronado Bay, surrounded by our families and a few close friends. We each wore pretty white dresses. We each wore girdles.

Adele says that whenever I get serious about politics or history or other people's mistakes—basically whenever I want to make a salient point—I make my "lecture face." My eyes stretch to the size of wall clocks and my forehead compresses. I've seen the wedding video: it's true. There I stand in a gown and high heels, tresses piled femininely atop my head, and yet my shoulders slump forward like a pitcher on the mound, my forehead crumples, and I become decidedly resolute as I recite my carefully composed vows:

> *"My love," I say.*
>
> *First, let's get the hard stuff out of the way: I promise to wipe down the counters and to be mindful of books and papers piling up by my side of the bed. I'll be a better sport. I'll try not to grumble and sigh so much when you beat me at Scrabble. And I promise to never again put 87-grade gasoline in your car.*
>
> *Now, to weightier matters: Here's what I know so far:*
>
> *I love you as I've never loved anything in all my life. And I knew I loved you instantly. There was no confusion, no weighing pros and cons, no settling for this thing because I was getting that thing, no wishing you looked or kissed or laughed or spoke just a little less or more like something or someone else. You were the one for me. You'll always be the one for me. Because of all the people in all the cities in all the world, you're my favorite.*
>
> *I like you as much as I love you: thoroughly. I care about what you think. I value your opinions on art and books and people and politics, and especially on me: on my work, my thinking, my risotto, my choices about what to do or say or wear. I love your perspective; the way you tell stories; the details you choose, the words you draw out, the way your hands move. You enliven the moment. You enchant. I get excited when I see your car. I still put on lipstick when I pull into the garage. I love to make you laugh. It's like a*

favorite hobby; it brings me nothing but comfort and pleasure. I want to make you laugh until we're old ladies, which will likely be next week. I love our life. I love you. And just as importantly, I respect you. Profoundly.

I have said that it's a hell of a lot of work being worthy of you, but I'm so much better for it. The high road is your first instinct. Kindness is just a reflex. You are so good to people, yet you manage to be true to yourself. The first night we met, you called your best friend Susie from the beach and said, "This date is going really well—I have a new girlfriend!" And then you put me on the phone with her. She said, "Adele House is the best girl in the whole world." She meant it literally. I think of that all the time when I watch you move through the world with such grace. You possess more moral clarity, more integrity than anyone I know. You're hopeful and warm, and then you're implausibly fun. And your dancing face just slays me.

I promise to continue working on me. I'm not as honest as you are, but I want to be. I don't always choose the high road, or the kindest road, but I want to. To admire the love of my life this much is the very meaning of prosperity. I promise to challenge myself; to be the best version of me that I can. I promise to listen to you, to admit when I'm wrong, to talk, to let you in, to be your rock and to allow you to be mine. I can promise these things because you are the best girl in the whole world. I happen to be the luckiest, and I know it. I also know that I'll love you for the rest of our lives, with a tenderness and a devotion that—if the last six years are any indication—will only grow deeper as the days and the years pass.

When I married Adele, I knew what I'd known since I was six: that I had one true love and that the convictions of at least this one romantic were undeniable.

During the reception, my father—a staunch Republican—raised a glass to toast our happiness. He's aware that our love is not a lifestyle choice. My lifestyle is like that of most Americans. I worry about my job; I watch the Super Bowl; I overcook the green beans on Thanksgiving. Dad wants for me what every parent wants for their child: a life rich with experience and love.

My mother is more practical. She knows that with or without a license, a marriage is a marriage is a marriage, and that when two people share their lives and their space, negotiations are key. That is exactly why my mother never remarried. She doesn't care to negotiate. She taught me that intransigence is like the nuclear option in a marriage. Something or someone has to give, and in our marriage, that's usually me.

For instance, recently I discovered a fork had fallen down the kitchen drain—not on the disposal side but the other side, the inaccessible no-man's-land of a drain. It must have been there for years. Adele had to lure the utensil, now fuzzy with basic evolution, up to the grate with a hanger. I then grabbed it with some pliers and wriggled it through the grate. I saw Baby Jessica emerging from the well, and as I bathed the poor fork in warm water, Adele stared at me as if I'd just had a psychotic break. "We're not keeping that fork."

I paused, still cradling it.

"I won't use that fork. I don't want it with the other forks."

I protested with a look—and this is a look I've perfected—that says, "Clearly, you are not in your right mind, but I will nevertheless be patient with you."

Within six seconds, it was clear that Adele had no intention of budging. I trudged to the pantry and dumped the fork on the morning's coffee grinds. In domestic battles, I surrender at the first sign of aggression. I know when to stand down. This is survival for me—the fork is on its own.

Adele picks her battles, too. She accepts that my desk can become a hazardous waste dump. She does not, however, accept that bills may be buried beneath receipts and magazines and packages of Dentyne; that's why bills go directly to her. We negotiated that settlement in couples counseling. In fact, we worked on our marriage long before it was legally a marriage.

I kill spiders; she cleans the cat box. I cook; she empties trash cans. And we're sensitive to one another's neuroses, like my washcloth hysteria. For some reason, maybe from being cleaned to death in a past life, I'm squeamish about people wringing out washcloths. She warns me before she cleans her face, so I can run away.

We have the same challenges any couple has: animals die, roofs leak—I even got sober after we met. But we also have the same comforts that any couple has: we hold hands at weddings and funerals. We are family. And our relatives are family, too.

When Papa—Adele's grandfather, who I adored as my own—had a stroke in 2008, we went down to San Diego from our home in Los Angeles to take bedside hospital shifts and do laundry. One morning, I volunteered to grocery shop. When I pulled into the Vons parking lot, I got stuck behind a woman's Volvo with a "YES on 8" bumper sticker. Proposition 8 was the measure that eliminated same-sex couples' rights to marry in California. When it passed later that November, Prop 8 had the disorienting affect of crushing our jubilation over electing the first black president.

Staring at this person's bumper, I felt attacked. This was personal. The stranger in that car felt that I shouldn't have the right to marry Adele, my person, my one true love, and she had no compunction about spitting on our marriage with her sticker.

Like most good couples, our devotion is not just about us. We make each other better as individuals and citizens. We contribute threads of stability to our families' fabric. And because we are better for having each other, we make our neighborhood and community and country a better place to live. It was sad that this stranger in her Volvo, who presumably enjoys her own stability inside a family, felt somehow threatened by our commitment.

Sitting there in my car, feeling maligned by her scorn, I remembered when gay marriage became a hot-button issue. The Massachusetts ruling had come down, which legalized—on constitutional grounds—same-sex marriage in that state. It was 2004 and religious conservatives were mounting their high horses. Right after the decision, Adele and I were down in San Diego, having dinner at my mother-in-law's house, discussing the social and legal ramifications with the family. Papa was a spry eighty-nine at the time and still had a sharp legal mind. He'd founded one of the top law firms in San Diego and had made it his life's mission to fight for people's civil rights. He'd advised the Hollywood Ten's defense (directors and writers who were blacklisted during the McCarthy era and had refused to name names), had advocated for social justice (when such positions were not at all popular), had spearheaded a pro bono lawyer program for the disadvantaged, and had generally lived with more honor and integrity than I thought was possible in mere mortals. Midway through the meal, the topic of domestic partnerships in California came up. Adele's brother asked, "Besides being able to say you're 'married,' what other rights are you guys being denied?"

"Isn't that enough?" Papa asked.

Indeed.

Both Adele's brother and I were speechless. I have never been so impressed in my life. While I had been lining up a litany of injustices, Papa cut cleanly to the marrow: is treating our devotion as "separate but equal" ultimately—is it basically—respectful?

Papa died on July 27, one week before the Supreme Court of California ruled Proposition 8 unconstitutional; we suspect that he pulled some strings.

When we heard that he was gone, I held Adele while she cried. Then later, when I was making tea and I fell apart, she held me. We will endure losses for the rest of our lives; it's part of being human; it's part of life, as is joy. We'll have each other. We'll get crushed, but these cataclysms will be more bearable; and when we win, the spark we feel will be more vivid. That's what true loves do. They enrich each other's existence. And who doesn't deserve to have that? Especially if you're lucky enough to find it.

Note to self:

Love has no downside;
honor it without question.

"I'm So Glad I Didn't Kill Myself Over What's-His-Name"

TRACEY JACKSON

Tracey Jackson has been a screenwriter for twenty years. A couple of her films are *The Guru* and *Confessions of a Shopaholic*. She also made the controversial documentary *Lucky Ducks*, which she wrote, produced, and directed. Her first book, *Between a Rock and a Hot Place*, a personal account of how fifty is not the new thirty, is being published by Harper-Collins in February 2011. She is a compulsive blogger on her website www.traceyjacksononline.com. Jackson lives in New York with her husband and two children.

There is no question the stories one likes to read about love are the ones with obviously happy endings: *We saw each other from across a crowded room and were together from that day forth. . . . We were seated next to each other on a plane, train, bus, or subway car that was broken and didn't move for two hours, and that's all it took for us to know this was it. . . . I was the maid of honor and he was the best man. . . . He was my boss, and yes, he was married, but nobody understood him like me. He was unhappy, but he took one look at me, and we both knew we had to spend the rest of our lives together.*

But the truth is, for every Cinderella ending, for every "I knew it from the moment I laid eyes on him" story, there are usually infinitely more *I thought he was perfect until . . .* moments, or *He was everything I wanted, but he didn't want me.* There are endless tales of "if only." Hours that turned into days, days that turned into weeks, weeks that turned into months, and sometimes even years that turned into decades, all the while lamenting the one who might have been the one who got away.

And then there are the handful of men who—at least in my case—make you sure it would be the end of the world if things didn't work out with them. Every woman has some. That date or encounter that we turn into a blank screen onto which we project all our romantic fantasies. A poor schmuck there for one dinner, who I managed to turn into my happily ever after, and—even more important—convince myself that if things didn't work out, if we did not walk down that aisle and into the sunset, then my life was over, finito, kaput.

It's only now, after living five decades and finding the love of my life in my late thirties, that I'm able to look back with some amount of perspective on all those hours spent sitting by the phone, crying myself to sleep and torturing my friends with inane questions like, "Do you think the fact that he said, 'See ya,' means he'll take me to Cabo for the weekend?"

Sometimes, I wish I had all that wasted time back. But then, I've also learned that it wasn't actually wasted; it's those wrong turns we thought would lead us to the right place that actually teach us where the right place is.

In my twenties, there was this one one-sided romance in

particular that I remember vividly, since for some reason it was the one that I felt would really do me in. I'd convinced myself that if I didn't marry this man (we'll call him Bill for the sake of this story), then my life would truly not be worth living.

Bill and I had been fixed up by my best friend, who was about to get married. There is no question that decades of therapy later, I can finally draw a connection to her happiness in finding Mr. Right to my convincing myself that Bill was my own Mr. Right. On paper, the place we tend to draw so much of our futures, Bill was perfect. Though he was a good fifteen years older than me, he was gorgeous, which is always a plus. He was also a successful film producer, nominated for an Academy Award during the year of my pining for him. He was funny, well traveled, well read, charming, and very nice—at least on the one date I had with him.

Yes, one date. We had one double date with my best friend and her fiancé, but that's all it took. One look at Bill and somehow I had decided, without question, that he was the one. During dinner, I ordered lamb chops, and so did he. Destiny? Then afterward, we split a dessert. Was that a sign or what? Double destiny?

We even slept together. Hey, it was the seventies.

By the time he left in the morning, I was beyond smitten. I wanted him to stay forever. But like Billy Crystal in *When Harry Met Sally*, he wanted to get home to his fab bachelor pad before I had even poured the coffee. As he walked out the door he said, "I'll call you."

I thought that meant an hour later. He meant: I will never see you again.

But I didn't take this lightly. When I want something, I always manage to convince myself that through a combination of single-mindedness, hard work, and perseverance, I can turn things my way. This character trait works in many areas of my life—love is not one of them. At twenty-two, I did not yet understand this.

None of my tactics was particularly original. I sat by the phone waiting for him to call while I pored over bridal magazines. I tortured my friend who fixed us up by making her relive every detail of the nine hours I spent with Bill, six of which were spent sleeping. Every word was examined for subtext, every gesture—from the way he drove home to the way he put on his pants—was ascribed a meaning.

I waited one week for him to call. One torturous week, where between the tears I convinced myself maybe he was away, or locked up closing a deal, or—since he lived alone—perhaps he slipped in the shower and cracked his head open and was bleeding to death at that exact moment. Maybe I should call? Maybe I shouldn't? What if I did? I could have written a novel in the time I spent debating this issue.

I finally gave in and called, but in that oh-so-fabulous way we all did back before caller ID and star 69. Immediately after he answered, I hung up; it was just enough to find out that he was indeed alive and well and simply ignoring me. This, of course, resulted in more nights of crying myself to sleep. But being an eternal, delusional optimist, I decided to take fate into my own hands. I would make this work. Besides, I had seen the perfect china for us the day before. I knew exactly what my bridesmaids would wear. I loved the name Ashley for our first child. I knew exactly what I would wear when I was on his arm for next year's Oscar ceremony.

If I wasn't contemplating suicide, I was planning our future and making up excuses why he had put our impending love affair and marriage on hold. Maybe he had to break up with someone else first. Perhaps he was cleaning out his closet to make room for my stuff. Maybe, maybe, maybe.

I had planned our entire future, including vacations, and he had forgotten my name.

I only know this because I finally got up the nerve to call and ask him to a dinner party. The only way I figured I could move this thing forward and order the damn china was to get him to know me better. So my best friend and I decided to plan a party and invite him. One more night spent with me and he too would be convinced we were destined to be the next "it couple"—our fate was sealed; he just needed to be the one to break the seal.

So I called him, and he picked up the phone. I had memorized his number already, as I was sure it was only a matter of months before it would be mine too. "It's Tracey," I said. Silence. "Tracey, from last week." His name had gone through my brain a minimum of fourteen times a minute since our date; but clearly he had pulled out of the driveway and never heard mine again.

"Right," he said. More silence.

I told him about the dinner. His response was that he was really busy. *My* response was "pick any night"; I cringe as I write this. He said he would get back to me.

He never did.

Though I got back to him like five times. I figured once a week for five weeks wasn't too much. But eventually he stopped taking my calls. I eventually caught on that he was not quite as convinced we were destined to be together as I was. This, of course, caused me to cry incessantly for months.

There's something about projected love gone wrong—which almost all projected love is bound to do—that really does you in. You only have the fabulous fictitious moments you've created yourself. You don't have the night he got drunk and tried to strangle your cat to bring you back to reality. Or the fact he wasn't so great in bed, was silent and withdrawn at the end of the day, hated your friends and family. Was self-involved, negligent, or irresponsible. No, you only have this perfect storybook romance you created and the happy ending you wrote before you filled in all the other details. This makes it very hard to admit it wasn't meant to be.

I literally took to my bed and cried for weeks. Sometimes I would venture out and drive by his house hoping to "run into him." Perhaps if he bumped into me the sparks he was clearly ignoring—perhaps out of fear of commitment?—would be ignited. Maybe?

I looked for his car all around town.

I bored my friends to death talking about him.

I cried some more.

I felt like my life was over.

I eventually went into therapy.

The therapist eventually explained many of my issues.

I eventually ran out of steam and had to accept that Bill and I would not be together. This took a good nine months, three of which were spent in tears, and the dramatic punctuation to the story was always: "I'm going to kill myself; I will never find anyone else."

After a year, I met someone who drove the same car, was in the same business and was just as good-looking, did the same thing with him. But this one didn't have quite the same intensity as the Bill episode. It would be hard for anyone to compete with Bill, the love of my life who was too stupid to figure it out.

Of course, I would go on to have many real relationships, and a marriage that had an expiration date stamped on it. And then, in my fourth decade, I would glance across a crowded room and find the love of my life.

I had two daughters, and when the first one started dating, she began to go through many of the same dilemmas and operatic impulses that I did. I would try to explain to her, thinking of Bill and several others, that these things just aren't what we think they are. Today, it feels like your entire life hinges on this guy's call, but you'll look back one day and realize it didn't matter one bit. Of course, she never believed me. You have to live it to understand it.

And then? Then the best thing happened. We were in a shop one day, in line and waiting to pay. I looked around at one point and couldn't help but notice a handsome older man behind me. I smiled, he smiled, and I went back to chatting with my daughter.

A moment later, someone came out and said a name: Bill's name. I turned around and looked at him again. Could it be? Is my memory that bad? It had only been thirty years

I went up to him, "Bill, it's Tracey Jackson." We did the usual "how are you's?" and "it's been so long's." I introduced him to my daughter, who was only four years younger than I was the last time I saw him, and we exchanged cards, promising we would have lunch one day soon to catch up on old times. Except the truth was, the only old times we had outside of that one dinner were the ones I fabricated in my head.

I put his card in my purse and paid for my purchases.

Then we got in the cab, and I turned to my daughter and said, "So, that guy in there?"

She nodded. "He was good-looking."

"Well, let me tell you something," I said. "I spent nine months wanting to kill myself because he wouldn't call me back. I was totally in love with him, convinced he was the answer to my life. And now, face-to-face with him, I didn't even know who he was."

She gave that look that only teens can give—part "I get it" and part "you're so weird, how can we be related?" There are some lessons that you have to learn for yourself.

I thought about Bill a lot that night. Were they wasted hours and days spent crying, or do we have to go through those steps as our rite of passage? There is truth to the old idiom that we have to kiss many frogs before we find our prince, even if that frog may be very handsome and might look like a prince on paper.

Still, we have to know the difference so we can spot the real prince from across the crowded room, or on the train, or now, I guess, online. The moral of this story is fairly clear: Don't torture yourself too much over these guys, as chances are that one day you won't even remember their names or their faces.

Oh, and by the way, he never called for that lunch!

Note to self:

Don't project love onto a person
who is not interested in a date,
much less a destiny.

Fragmented Pieces

JACLYN KATZ

Jaclyn Katz graduated high school in New York City in 2010, and started at Brown University in the fall of the same year. She plans to concentrate on political science and hopes to write for her college newspaper as well as continue her own literary work.

For eight years, I had a so-called normal family as characterized by much of the outside world. If someone were to look at my family today—which consists of two fathers, a sister, and four pets—it might seem different; maybe even strange. Yet before I even turned ten years old, I learned that the way a family looks externally has nothing to do with the love on the inside.

As a child, I thought all families looked like my "normal" family. However, while I was nowhere near worldly enough to imagine the kind of "unconventional" family to which I now belong, I was able to grasp that my family was unhappy. I loved the individuals within my family, but as a unit, we didn't function. No love bound us together, and a tragedy ultimately tore us apart.

Through the tragic experience, I learned that love is like energy in that it can neither be created nor destroyed; it can only be transformed from one state to another. The love I have for my mother and sister was never destroyed; my love just transformed as my family changed forms. And though a tragedy of the magnitude that I experienced could have easily caused me to give up on love altogether, I didn't lose my capacity to love; in fact, I've realized that love—not blood—is what ties a family together.

It is hard for me to make sense of my memories from before the tragedy. Some of them seem insignificant, and I don't know why my mind chose those moments over other ones to store. The pieces together make no coherent sense. I guess you could attribute my muddled memories to trauma, or even just age—after all, I was only eight years old when everything changed.

Of course, I remember the last piece: The Last Day. I consider that to be in a different psychological dimension altogether. Visions from The Last Day come back to me in the middle of dreams, or sometimes, even when I'm perfectly awake. My mind goes soaring somewhere else, and suddenly there it is, happening all over again in front of me.

I wish I could make sense of the pieces I remember. Maybe then, the "before" part of my life would not seem so distant and distinct. If I could somehow put them in order, then perhaps my life would not feel so broken. But I can't. When I look back on it, that period of my life seems like it never happened to me. The person in those memories is not the same one telling this story. I call her "Old Me," which is ironic, since she is actually a young me. I was only a child.

Old Me lived in a picturesque redbrick house on top of a hill that was perfect for sledding. My family's house was the biggest and most beautiful on a cul-de-sac called Ivy Court, with a pool and tennis court to boot. Now, if I picture it, a shiver runs down my spine.

We might have looked like the perfect family: one father (a doctor, no less!), one mother (a periodontist!), and three beautiful girls. The situation inside the house, however, was disastrous. Though I was young, I knew that Mommy and Daddy fought more than the average Mommy and Daddy. Daddy frightened me, because he changed moods so erratically that I would never know if he was Nice Daddy or Angry Daddy at any given moment. I had a feeling that he frightened Mommy, too. As the oldest of three siblings, I tried not to let the fighting bother me, and I wanted to protect my younger sisters from feeling scared and threatened. I hid behind a mask of strength, when really, I constantly felt vulnerable within those redbrick walls.

When Mommy and Daddy weren't getting along, Mommy would take my sisters and me out of the house. We'd go somewhere innocent: a pizza place, Friendly's, a diner. My younger sisters, Alli and Kim, thought the excursions were fun, but when I looked at Mommy, I knew something was wrong. There was something sad in her smile.

By the time we arrived back home, Daddy would have changed. He'd become nice and sweet, and sometimes he had presents waiting. He would kiss and hug us; I'd go along with it, but I didn't like it. I didn't trust him. He had changed moods so quickly. I thought there must be something artificial in his affection.

My last excursion with Mommy, Alli, and Kim was all the way to Arizona. My father did not come on the trip with us.

We went over Christmas break to visit my grandfather and his wife, Shirley. I later learned that it wasn't intended to be a vacation. The week we went to Arizona was the week Mommy decided that she was leaving Daddy—that she wasn't ever going back to him.

But she did go back. And the next week she was gone forever.

On the cold December night we arrived home from Arizona, Mommy got mad that Daddy had bought milk when we already had some in the fridge. (That's how I remember it anyway, though that doesn't seem like something my mom would argue about. I'm probably wrong about the cause of the argument, but the point is something set her off.) I'm not sure what happened next or how it all escalated, but suddenly I saw Daddy twisting Mommy's wrist and then snapping her glasses in two. My mask of strength fell apart the moment I saw my mother in pain, and I started crying. I remember Alli and Kim started crying when they saw my tears. I don't know what happened after that, but it was a terrible homecoming.

Unlike in most familial situations where the possibility of divorce causes the child anxiety, I was looking forward to the day when Grandma, Mommy, Alli, Kim, and I would move to a little house in Princeton Park, a neighborhood near my elementary school. It would be the Girls' House. I pictured everything: walking to school with Grandma, and eating her noodle pudding every night. I pictured Mommy smiling without any sadness in her eyes. I pictured not seeing Daddy ever again.

None of those images came true. On January 6, 2001, my life changed forever. It was The Last Day I was Old Me.

My bipolar father committed suicide by sitting in a car with the engine on. The gas seeped into my house, killing my mother and my almost-six-year-old sister.

The End.

I'm told that my interpretation of that day is wrong. People say that I fell unconscious and had to be shipped to the hospital in an airplane. I believe this to be false, though, because I clearly, vividly remember that day. I remember the dialogue. And I remember the faces, dead and alive.

I'm also the only person who can say what went on inside the house. Other people conjecture why Mommy and Alli headed to the basement that morning, which was the closest area to the toxic fumes. People guessed, and presented their inklings as truths in newspapers and magazines. But I know the truth.

I remember waking up early that Saturday morning in the beautiful house on Ivy Court. The first thing I noticed was that every room smelled really funky and gassy. I didn't think much of it. I was too excited—Mommy had told us the day before that we were going to make the goody bags for Alli's upcoming karate-themed birthday party, and I couldn't wait to get started.

Alli woke up and as we waited to make the goody bags we played with Rescue Heroes and Barbie dolls. Though I was quite the bossy and aggressive older sibling, we were still incredibly close; she wasn't only my sister—she was my best friend. When Alli and I went to Mommy's room after a while to see if she was ready, we found our two-year-old sister Kim sitting on the bed with her pacifier and blanket. Mommy was there, too, but she left to go do something. I don't remember her last words to me.

Alli and I watched some baby shows on TV with Kim for a bit, but soon returned to our dolls. After playing for a while, I felt like I couldn't breathe, and I told Alli to run and get Mommy. This is the part of the story that comes soaring back to me all the time. A visceral shaking takes over when my mind recalls it without my permission. I wish I were the one to get Mommy.

But I made Alli go downstairs to find Mommy, and she never came back up.

After a while waiting for Alli, I went downstairs myself. I couldn't find Alli on the first floor, so I headed toward the basement, where the door to the garage was located. It was already open, and I saw tons of cars outside on our driveway.

In our garage, there was only one car. Daddy was inside of it and he looked like he was sleeping with his mouth slightly open, eyes closed. Then I saw Mommy. She was wrapped in her towel. When the gas overwhelmed her, she must have fallen, and the towel had slipped below her chest, exposing her breasts. I remember averting my eyes.

I didn't see Alli.

I recall being put into a van with Kim, who was screaming. I didn't know what was going on. Then, a woman asked me to get out of the van, and she quickly laid Kim and me on one of those rolling hospital mattresses. She covered us with blankets, as it was a cold January morning, and I was wearing only a nightshirt that hardly covered my bottom.

This is where certain details come back to me, and that's how I know I could never have gone on some airplane or fallen unconscious. I remember a couple of hospital workers rolling the mobile mattress down our long, snow-covered hill, and one of them saying, "We have to use more blankets. They can't get pneumonia."

I also remember going to the hospital in an ambulance, still sitting on the mattress with Kim, the hospital workers poking and prodding us with needles. Once we arrived, they rolled us into a waiting area behind a curtain, where I got an IV. (I didn't know what it was at the time, and I screamed and cried. I'm horrible with pain, still.) I recall an important-looking woman asking me if I had family on Long Island and if I knew their phone numbers. I told her about Grandma, and I recited the number, proud I had remembered it like Mommy had taught me.

Kim and I were put in the children's part of the hospital. For a long time, I had no idea what had happened. I kept telling people at the hospital that I had never made a doctor's appointment, and that today I was supposed to be making goody bags. The nurses just chuckled and told me I was cute.

Eventually, Grandma arrived. She looked empty, but relieved to see us. I told her I was excited because Alli and I were making goody bags today. She didn't say anything.

After a quick visit with Grandma, Kim and I were left alone for a little bit. We played video games in our beds, and I kept asking the nurse who checked on us where my mommy and sister were. She said they were at a different hospital. I asked why we were at hospitals when we were healthy, but she just chuckled again. I hated that nurse.

Then my maternal uncle, Bruce, my grandfather, and his wife, Shirley, arrived and they all sat around Kim and me on the hospital beds. They looked disheveled and heartbroken. Actually, they looked worse than that. But there is no way to describe it.

I don't remember exactly how the conversation started, but I remember the moment when I found out. Bruce said he had to tell us something about Mommy and Alli. Just like that, I knew. I was eight years old and I knew that Mommy and Alli were never coming back. My heart felt like it was engulfed in flames.

When Bruce told us, I looked up at the ceiling and screamed: "What!" I don't know why I chose that word. I felt like I was going to vomit. Kim had no idea what was going on, but patted my back and wiped away my furious tears. She said, "It's okay." I said it wasn't okay, Kim. I told her Mommy and Alli were gone. *Gone.* My hysteria started making her upset, but she still didn't understand the situation. She never felt the kind of pain or loss I felt. She still doesn't. I envy her for that reason.

Questions started racing through my head. Where would I live? Who would I live with? What was to become of my life? Where was my mom? It was all like some sort of weird dream. Something like this could never happen to me. This stuff didn't *actually* happen to people. Only to people on the news. Not to me. Not in a quiet, wealthy suburb.

Almost immediately after The Last Day, my living situation became sticky, to say the least. My grandfather and Shirley moved in with Kim and me at the Ivy Court house. So did my grandma—the former wife of my grandfather and former best friend of his wife. The Ivy Court house thus continued to be tense, but this new tension didn't frighten me. It was nothing compared to what I had witnessed before.

Still, no one thought living in that house was healthy, and it was only a matter of time until a new solution was worked out. When I arrived home from my first time at sleep-away camp that summer of 2001, the camp my mother and I had picked out together almost one year before, Ivy Court was no longer my home. My mother's brother, Bruce, moved with my sister and me to a house nearby, in a community called The Hamlet. That's when I learned that Bruce had voluntarily stepped up to be Kim's and my new parent. Our new house was in the same school district as the old one, and I started fourth grade with as much stability in my life as possible, given the circumstances. And though I still saw my grandparents all the time, admittedly, it was nice not living with them.

That same month, I met Bruce's new boyfriend, Steven. The first time I met him, he rolled into our new house on Rollerblades. He was amazing: sarcastic, funny, and positive. Steven was a much-needed source of relief and light. Sometimes, he still jokes that he's "the outsider," the only one not related to the three of us by blood (other than Belle and Kayla, our dogs, and Samantha and Lola, our cats, of course). But he has no idea how much Bruce, Kim, and I need him.

Steven moved into our house in The Hamlet sometime in 2002, and Kim and I became the adoptive daughters of both Bruce and Steven. Our new family was complete.

I didn't quite understand what Bruce and Steven's relationship was at the time—I really didn't think much about it—until a peer of mine informed me, unsolicited. He said my new parents were "gay." I didn't know what "gay" was, but somewhere along the way, negative connotations had lodged themselves into my child-mind. I asked Bruce and Steven about it, and they explained. I didn't understand exactly what they were saying, but they still managed to make me feel better, and after that it never became an issue.

It may sound implausible, but my new living situation never

struck me as odd. I never thought, *Why do I have these two men adopting me, calling themselves my new parents?* And although I missed calling someone "Mommy" or "Daddy" (I tried for a while with Bruce and Steven, but no names ever stuck) and sometimes felt left out when I saw my friends with their mothers, I would *never* want a replacement for my mother. If Bruce were straight and had a wife, I would probably despise her.

After I graduated elementary school the following year, we moved to New York City. Bruce and Steven felt our family would be more accepted there, and I did feel more comfortable in the liberal and urban environment. Though people are still curious, and love to ask me about Bruce and Steven. Who's tougher? Who yells more? Who's your favorite? Perhaps they're trying to find out who is more "Mommy-like" and who is more "Daddy-like," but I find those questions ridiculous.

I don't have a "favorite father." I don't go to Bruce with my personal problems instead of Steven, and I don't ask Steven for permission to stay out later instead of Bruce. I feel comfortable talking to both of them about everything. Of course, when I was twelve or thirteen, there were certain subject matters I needed Grandma for, but other than that, I go to either or both of them with all my problems. I think I have the best of both worlds: they discipline me and guide me like parents, but they listen to me and laugh with me like friends. And we love each other like family. We *are* family. Someday, when I become a parent, I hope my child feels as comfortable approaching me as I do with Bruce and Steven. I don't want negativity or secrets, and I don't want to come off as intimidating. I want to be my child's parent and friend. I hope my future spouse and I can create the same type of relaxed, humor-filled, and easygoing atmosphere that's present in my house; I hope my spouse and I can have the same type of unconditional love I know Bruce and Steven share.

Having lived with both a "typical" and an "atypical" family, I understand that exteriors have absolutely nothing to do with normalcy, contentment, or love. Love doesn't always look the way you think it should. Comfort and trust are abundant in my current household—they were absent in the house on Ivy Court.

Our family is so close-knit that sometimes it is difficult for me to fathom that I once had another family (and a dysfunctional one, to say the least). Still, it scares me that I only remember bits and pieces from that time of my life. I don't remember what my mother or sister *feel* like. I can't hear their voices or recall their scents.

Every day takes me farther away from the fragmented pieces of my childhood, and every day I will remember less and less. But I feel like if I write down my story now, the pieces will survive forever. Stories are eternal, and the characters within those stories live on. Mommy and Alli will remain alive in my writing.

I'm also writing this for Kim. For better or worse, she doesn't have any fragmented pieces. I know these pages won't give her a sense of who her mother and sister were, but I hope they will give her a sense of the magnitude of what happened to our family. A magnitude she can't feel under her skin like I can.

I cannot and will not ever forget how much I love my mother and sister. Though I only knew them for the first eight years of my life, they have shaped who I am indefinitely. They're not only in my thoughts—they're in *me*, always. I carry my memories of them with me wherever I go. I know my bond with them is the strongest, most intense kind of love I will ever experience.

To this day, I follow my mother's rules. She taught me how to be organized and studious; every day when I came home from school, it was homework first, play later. I don't think I would have maintained a 4.0 GPA in high school without her, nor is it likely that I'd be starting college at Brown University in the fall of 2010 without the work ethic she imparted.

My sister, Alli, showed me that boys and girls can do the same things. For whatever reason, Alli walked around our house topless much of the time. (Sorry, Alli, if you'd be embarrassed by this now.) I thought it was odd, but she taught me that it doesn't matter what people think, so long as you are content. She was an athlete, a budding soccer star. I'm telling you: she would have gone places.

I don't really know how to make sense of the pieces. I don't know why it was me who survived. I was the bossiest older sibling ever, and a rather loud-mouthed child. I was probably the most obnoxious one of the bunch. I'm not saying I'm not grateful that I survived or that I think I should have died. I'm just questioning whoever made the decision that I would be the one to live.

I know one thing, however—I wouldn't be who I am now without going through that experience, which makes me think: Who would I be if it never happened? Where would I live? Would I be as savvy without my New York City wit? Would I care about politics? Would I sing? What would I be when I grew up? Where would my life end?

I can ask an infinite amount of questions, but unfortunately I'll never know, because unfortunately, it all happened. All I know is that my life went up in smoke, and from the ashes, I was reborn again into something new. With a family now bound by trust, understanding, and love, I've learned that it is possible to pick up the fragmented pieces of your past, and create a bright future.

Note to self:

Your family shapes who you are,
and, if you're lucky,
teaches you how to love,
even after they're gone.

New Moon

HEATHER KRISTIN

Before writing for *Glamour, The Huffington Post,* and *Slate,*
Heather Kristin was home-schooled with her twin sister in
Hell's Kitchen, New York. Her unpublished novel *Brooklyn to
Bombay* was a finalist for the Amazon Breakthrough Novel
Award. She's a fourth-year mentor at Girls Write Now, a non-
profit that matches at-risk teens with women writers, and is
currently working on a memoir.

Late one November a few years back, I returned home
from a month in Spain with my borderline obsessive, now
ex-boyfriend Tavio feeling exhausted beyond my twenty-nine
years. I'd wanted to have what I can now identify as an *Eat,
Pray, Love* transformative experience; instead, I'd returned to
my twelve foot-by-twelve-foot studio apartment a block from
Central Park the same mixed-up, jobless person I'd been
when I left. The floor was cluttered with six years' worth of
self-help workbooks, journals, and Broadway musical song-
books. I had no furniture except for a mattress on the floor,
one bookshelf I found next to the garbage on 72nd Street, and a

mini-refrigerator that was the base for a two-burner stove and sink. I'd always meant to buy more stuff, but my various jobs waitressing, cocktailing, catering parties, coat-checking, being a nanny, teaching violin, standing in for Kristin Davis on *Sex and the City*, and playing myself on a low-paying reality TV show had kept me too busy running in circles like a gerbil to find the time. Looking out my window, I peeked through the fire escape to the outline of luxury buildings beyond and wondered if my life would ever be stable and if I'd ever find love.

The phone rang, distracting me from my thoughts. I let my answering machine pick up so I could screen the call.

"Wanna come to a party for vegetarians, poets, and Buddhists? Afterwards we could have our Tarot cards done," said my friend Jill, a fiftysomething, single mother. A few years back, I had bumped into her and reconnected (we had lost touch for about five years while I was traveling to various foreign countries) at the Ninth Avenue Food Festival. The first time I met Jill, I was ten, and my family had recently been evicted from our railroad flat, leaving us homeless for one year. "Call me back. The reading could change your life." *Click.*

I thought about picking up the phone as her words echoed back: *change your life.* Instead, I lit up a smoke, and pressed the button next to the red blinking light on the answering machine. A guy I'd had a one-night stand with a few months ago had left a message. So had my mom in Ohio. She said she was busy taking care of my grandparents and how much she hated her life. I pressed delete, fighting the urge to pick up the phone and tell her she never should've left the rent-controlled apartment my twin and I spent our teen years in and moved back to her hickish hometown.

The phone rang again.

"One more thing: I hope you broke up with that guy. I don't care if he was the best musician in the world, he was too much drama," Jill told my machine.

I picked up.

"Yes, he and I are done," I assured her while nervously scratching the back of my neck. "When and where's the party?"

"On Christopher Street. Tonight," Jill said.

I told her I couldn't go. It was too short of notice. I had nothing to wear. I hadn't taken a shower. I wasn't hungry. Excuses, excuses. What I didn't tell her was that it was the first time I'd been without a boyfriend in a long while and I wanted to stay home and stuff myself with handfuls of cereal, finger-lick a whole jar of Nutella, shove spoonfuls of ice cream into my mouth—fill the hole, and then release it all in reverse order, with everything swimming in creamy swirls.

But Jill didn't take no for an answer and before I knew it I was standing on an apartment terrace overlooking Manhattan, with the Empire State Building glowing above the rest of the city. All around, partygoers clinked glasses together; some pointed to the moon slowly eclipsing in the sky. I felt empty as the sky darkened.

In the corner nearby, a couple kissed passionately. I watched as the girl, who was sitting on the guy's lap, stopped and whispered something in a foreign language. Next to them, a puffy-lipped guy stood smoking.

"Do you have an extra one?" I asked.

He nodded and pulled one out.

"I'm quitting soon," I added.

"No judgments."

"Are you a Buddhist?"

"No, but I play one on TV. Kidding. I spent part of my child-hood in a commune with my mom. The other part was with my dad in Louisiana, and then I went to boarding school."

Off and on for the next few hours, Zack, my partner-in-smoking, brought me glasses of wine. I learned that the event wasn't actually a Buddhist, vegetarian, poetry party, but a birth-day celebration for a young Indian girl, and that Jill was Zack's mother's eccentric cousin who often misunderstood invites. As the moon turned black, Zack asked about my family. I told him that I'd been so young when my adoring and unstable mother informed me about my missing father that I had believed every story she spun about him. At first, she said he'd died in a car accident overseas while she was pregnant with my twin sister and me. Next she'd read from the Bible about how Jesus was im-maculately conceived, and allowed me to convince myself that the big man in the sky was my father. Then he was a TWA airline pilot who died in a crash. As I grew tired of fairy tales in my teen years, she began to say he was a spy for the Danish government and if he wanted to find us he could.

Zack smiled and said, "Sounds like she had a few secrets. You have any?"

I smiled vaguely and scratched the back of my neck as I in-haled his scent through our shared cigarette. I imagined telling him everything: my troubled past, the addictions, the desire to change my life. He stepped closer, and his eyes shone as the moon became full again.

"Would you like to go ice-skating sometime?" I blurted out.

"Sure," Zack replied, looking half bewildered, half pleased.

I silently noted that my mother took us ice-skating in Central Park before we lost our home and after a government agency found us an apartment in a Hell's Kitchen tenement. I wanted to return to the rink where I had seen the glittering buildings peeking between trees and dreamed of living steps away from the Boat Pond, before everything became so complicated.

Jill signaled from across the half-empty room. "Let's go," she mouthed. I handed Zack my telephone number, he helped me with my coat, and Jill and I left the party together.

"He has a crush on you. I saw it in his eyes," Jill said, as we rushed down the chilly sidewalk.

"No he doesn't. And he's not my type. He seems like he'd make a good friend."

We entered a Tarot card reader's storefront. The Gypsy lady placed the cards and read them; I handed her twenty bucks. Ten minutes later, back on the street corner, I couldn't remember what she had predicted for my future.

"You're smitten!" Jill said.

When I returned to my studio apartment, I lay down on my mattress on the floor and pulled out my journal. As I flipped to a blank page, out fell a snapshot from my childhood. In it I was eight years old, had two long braids, and was playing violin on the corner of 53rd Street and Fifth Avenue. I remembered watching the school buses pass while I performed for money so my family could eat. I remembered being hungry for hours and lying about my age to tourists as the years went by so they'd hand me five-dollar bills; they gave me more money if they thought I was younger. I remembered gaining weight from the free block of government orange cheese the church handed out on Saturdays and thinking I should try to stay small so people would think I was cute and plucky.

That was when it hit me. I was a young woman, not a wounded little girl seeking people's approval. I couldn't live in the past anymore, nor could I change it. But I could change my mind-set toward it. I wrote in my journal: *I have the power to grow and love. Today I become mindful of my thoughts and actions.* I continued writing those words down every day until a week had passed and I hadn't binged.

Zack called the following week and I stalled in setting up a date. My heart raced as I tried to hold on to both him and myself, knowing I couldn't do both. I needed to learn how to love myself before I could love someone else. But he called again and sounded so gentle, so kind that I agreed to dinner.

"The student film I'm working on is running late," I said into the payphone on the night we'd agreed to meet. "I can't see you tonight."

Minutes later the director called wrap and I walked home. I felt guilty for not calling Zack back, but I knew that if I didn't have a few more weeks of releasing the pain of the past and being present with myself, I'd slip and be staring at my puke in the clear plastic cup, trying to figure out how I got to this place and blaming someone else for my failings. I had to keep journaling, writing down my commitment to grow up and find out who I was, and not put my hopes in a romance that might not work out.

The next day, I called Zack and told him I was getting over a toxic relationship (with myself, but I didn't say this), and asked if we could just be friends. He agreed and invited me to dinner downtown at Café Noir. I met him the following night wearing a turtleneck and jeans. Throughout dinner I kept scratching the back of my neck, trying to dig out the ugly parts, and then crossing my arms in front of me. But I couldn't take my eyes off of him. After dinner he didn't try to kiss me. Instead, we walked a short block to the subway entrance and paused, looking at the moon watching over us.

Once we were on the uptown C train, Zack asked how I knew Jill.

"When I was ten years old, my family was evicted from our apartment. We lost everything. We traveled the city streets homeless for one year. One day we met a woman who invited us into her apartment. She had a couple of kids, and Jill was the babysitter. Jill and I have known each other off and on for twenty years."

"So, if you hadn't been homeless, I never would have met you?"

"Seems everything happens for a reason," I said.

"Do you think we were destined to meet?"

"Let's take it one day at a time," I said, thinking of my addictions, and how my family and I had survived for so many years.

The train came to a halt.

"Fourteenth Street's my stop," Zack said, rising, and then in one final swoop, he leaned over and kissed my forehead. No one had ever done that before. Somehow I knew then that I had met a person who would wait for me, who would show me love with no expectations.

Zack and I continued to see each other through the holidays. We met for casual lunches, went to museums, danced tango in his living room, talked on the phone late at night, and listened to Edith Piaf sing for hours. I didn't need a different body to experience this new life so I stopped sneaking food and hiding my emotions. I was getting stronger.

A few months later, I awoke in Zack's Brooklyn apartment to my outline of sweat on the sheets. The night before I had confessed everything to him: my anxiety about not having enough money, how I learned to binge and purge before dropping out of college, my history of poor relationships, my lack of commitment to boyfriends, my low self-esteem, and how I had recently traded my sleeping and eating disorder for self-harm—another old trick. I showed Zack the scabs on the back of my neck and detailed how I dug my fingernail into my flesh until it bled. He asked how it all began and I told him it had started at age ten as a way to distract myself from the shame of using food stamps at the local bodega. I explained how, as long as I had these harmful external actions to perform, I didn't have to focus on my internal life. Plus they were addictions, and just like my childhood, I had no control over them.

As I slowly stretched out in bed, remembering our conversation, Zack entered his bedroom with coffee and toast for me. He brushed the hair off my sticky forehead, feeling my warmth, and kissed me. I looked into his eyes and promised to stop starving, binging, purging, and punishing myself.

"You were put on this earth for so much more," he whispered in my ear, taking my hand off my neck, and kissed me again and again.

With each kiss, I was getting a taste of love and I wanted to experience even more. I had to trust that he wouldn't leave me like other boyfriends if I looked him in the eye and said, "I need help."

"I'll stand by you as you figure things out," he said.

I studied his face—Zack has this smile that is very soft and warm—and wondered if I could fix myself. We talked a while;

he shared some of his intimacy issues and listened to mine like no one else had and held me tight in his arms, our bodies one.

"When I was growing up in the Zen Center, we ate brown rice," Zack said. "I knew other kids were living different lives on the outside. Sometimes I wanted to eat handfuls of potato chips, but that wasn't an option. They didn't have junk food or big juicy steaks lying around. So I learned how to be present and mindful. You have to be kind to your body as well as your heart."

"I don't know how. I feel like such a failure; I keep promising to start over, only to relapse or find a new addiction," I said.

"Stop judging yourself."

"I want to be a better person," I said.

"That's your ego talking. Stop trying to control everything and let go."

Zack seemed so different from me, so confident and grounded. I wasn't sure if we were a perfect fit, but his eyes reflected back the same desire to evolve.

As he got up, I felt his shape imprinted on the mattress. I rolled onto his side of the bed, let my body merge into his outline, and felt whole.

The next day, something changed inside of me. Food, fame, and my family were never going to save me and I didn't want Zack to be burdened with playing guru superhero. I knew I had to go to therapy and learn how to navigate my life without those daily crutches. After a few months, I came to the realization that there would be no magic in healing, no quick fix. I had to just stop self-destructing and be compassionate to myself and others. Simple as that.

Around our second anniversary of that fateful night when

the moon eclipsed and we first laid eyes on each other, we quit smoking, and I stopped hurting myself. There came a moment when those destructive behaviors lost their power. As I worked on myself and began to recover, Zack and I grew closer. Together, we tore down walls and became even more passionate about life. The time had come to know the truth about ourselves, to delve deep into our hearts, to feel how big they could be, how far we could go, and to take a leap of faith that everything would be okay. I began to see that I did not begin and end at my skin. It was time to heal and forgive. Time to love and be loved.

The following spring, Zack and I got married at his half brother's château in France and I felt filled with more love than I ever dreamed possible. Seven years after our first meeting, we had a beautiful baby daughter we named Daisy Neoma. Her middle name means "New Moon."

For us, it means that every night can have a new beginning.

Note to self:

**Sometimes, by letting go
you can gain everything.**

Giving Voice

SHARON LAWRENCE

Over the years Sharon Lawrence has had a multifaceted career on stage and screen. Her characters have ranged from a
confident assistant district attorney in *NYPD Blue* to a stay-at-
home prostitute in *Desperate Housewives*, a murderous
realtor on *Monk*, a sociopathic serial killer on *Law & Order*,
Izzie's uneducated mother on *Grey's Anatomy*, and Velma
Kelly in *Chicago* on Broadway. As the former chair of the
Women in Film Foundation, Sharon managed their respected
film-finishing fund, sponsored by Netflix. As a women's health
advocate she supports the National Breast Cancer Coalition
and as an environmental activist she works with Global Green
and is a founding board member of Greenwish. You can learn
more by visiting www.sharon-lawrence.com.

I recently heard a story on the radio that confirmed
something I'd been thinking about. The woman who has been
the voice of Minnie Mouse for the past thirty years was discussing her life's work and the loss of the love of her life, her husband, the man who was the voice of Mickey Mouse for the same

thirty years. They met and fell in love in a recording studio playing those characters. Can't you just hear them now?

Lately, I have been very aware of the power of voices—in particular, my mother's. On the occasion of my parents' fiftieth wedding anniversary, one of her friends told me how grateful she is that my mom has become a regular visitor to her elderly mother, who is suffering from dementia and most likely Alzheimer's disease. Although a stranger, Mom's presence seems to reassure this frail woman, who is often confused and depressed. Perhaps it is Mom's experience as a caregiver for her own mother, who passed away with the disease known as "the long goodbye," or her natural gift for making vulnerable people feel at ease, which made my mother's contribution so effective. Both of those qualities come into play, I'm sure, but this friend also identified something about my mom that I heard as a deep truth: she has a remarkable voice. And if it soothes a soul who barely knows her, imagine the effect it has on those she loves.

It's not simple to describe a voice, but I will try. My mother's natural tone is pleasantly feminine yet not girlish. Her timbre is clear and rich. The slight Southern touches suggest ease and relaxation, rather than anxiety and tension, which can be associated with some heavy Southern drawls.

Voices are like personalities, they are produced by nature and nurture. Nature was kind to many of her physical attributes, and I suspect her long graceful neck offers an anatomical advantage also: this design permits longer vocal cords, allowing a greater range of tones and textures. As for nurture, both her parents had typical Smoky Mountain accents and slow, patient speech. From what I can manage to remember, their voices were neither especially offensive nor pleasant, but the overall effect of their gentle speech was significantly nurturing, and she echoed that quality. Since nature graced her with the ear of a musician, but not the soul of a performer, the pleasant sound of her voice is enhanced by the authenticity of her spirit coming through this instrument of expression.

As I reach a fiftieth milestone of my own, I realize how much I love that voice and how it has affected me. If I sound biased, I can't really argue that point. I'm fairly convinced that hers is the first voice I ever heard. (And yes, I know the story of the lost peasant child, who when asked by the villagers what his mother—the plainest of women—looked like, replied that she was most beautiful woman in the world.) But, like many of you, I grew up listening to Julie Andrews as Mary Poppins, and later Julie Kavner as Marge Simpson, so I know the difference. Mom's voice is special, and considering that we descend from humble mountain people whose twang is notorious, the beauty in her voice is a bit of an anomaly.

Although her physical beauty has always been recognized, to the rest of the world, my dad is the one with the voice. They actually met because of their voices, while singing in choir at college. She says his voice was what first attracted her to him. Dad went on to become a professional reporter and announcer with an impressive, even intimidating voice, which many people comment on to this day. His voice has always defined him in the world. But a mother's voice has special powers, and mine uses hers well.

When I was young, she sang to my brother and me all the time. She loves the feeling of singing. Early on she recognized that her musical ear had been inherited by me, so she taught me to harmonize, encouraged me to join choirs, and introduced me to great choral music. She herself sang in the church choir, and when the extended family gathered for Christmas, her crystalline soprano always sparkled and filled me with pride.

She nurtured my gift and instilled in me a confidence that has been instrumental in my path as an actress and advocate. Mom and I never really argued or went through a typical period of mother/daughter conflict. She was a sturdy, constant presence and would never choose to speak harshly or use coarse language. So, if something was wrong, I heard it in her voice—like the time she transformed in front of our very eyes.

My dad raced sports cars for fun in his mid-twenties, and my mother, brother, and I loved going to the weekend races. It was good, informal family fun, but one sunny day we watched as my father had a dramatic wreck on a red clay track in rural Virginia. Hearing Mom's horrified shriek was enough to verify my suspicions that it was bad. I had never heard a sound like that come out of her, and while the cloud of red dust still obscured the wreckage, she shifted into high gear. We had a dirt bike we'd brought with us into the infield, and although I had never seen her ride it, in a matter of moments we were all three mounted on that Yamaha 150—my five-year-old brother on the tank in front steadied by her gripping thighs, and seven-year-old me straddled behind her, arms wrapped firmly around her waist wondering how she had become Superwoman. In an unusually commanding voice she instructed us to "hold on!" and we were off, bounding through the infield filled with race teams and spectators, and made it over a creek in time to watch Dad climb out of his wrecked vehicle and walk away from the accident.

Typical of a guy in his twenties, Dad refused emergency medical treatment, but after an uncomfortable sleepless night, he rode home with us to Charlotte stretched out in the back of our station wagon. Mom knew he was more injured than he would admit and she instructed us to speak only in whispers on the long drive home so as not to disturb him. Our near silence spoke volumes, and when I returned from school the next day to find Dad in a neck brace supporting his broken vertebrae, my anxiety was mercifully calmed that night by the comforting and familiar sound of their low voices coming from their darkened bedroom.

The tone of my mom's sensible response to that dramatic episode in our lives left a big impression on me, and to this day, I am solid in a crisis. Don't get me wrong, Mom was not a stoic. Sometimes her voice would belie an undercurrent of something—frustration, anger, fear, feelings mothers don't often express to kids—I never even suspected.

When I was twelve years old, we moved for the first time to a new house, and as we were packing up the kitchen, I heard Mom utter a curse word for the first time. Nothing major had happened, only a tear in a plastic bag, but the "Damn it!" she emitted was stunning. She was high on a ladder holding the failed bag that had been used to cover a seldom-used wedding gift—a silver pitcher, I'll never forget it—stored in a remote cabinet. It was shocking for me to hear my mild-mannered mother curse, especially over something so small. But of course it wasn't small at all. Now that I have had to haul the artifacts of my life to different locations I understand how overwhelming moving can be. Her embarrassed apology made it clear that this move was more stressful for her than I realized, and her curse, her "Damn it!" provided my first recognition of subtext, a psychological complexity every good actor utilizes.

Because they believed in my abilities, my parents both supported my decision to pursue a career in theater. When I moved to New York City after graduation, long before cell phones kept people in constant touch, our weekly calls were what connected us. Although she never complained that I had made such a big move, the way she answered: "Sharon . . . ? " revealed an insecurity I remember noting. It was as if she was testing the truth of my safety in that strange city and wasn't sure the phone line could be trusted right away, that this expensive luxury of long-distance calling might be a mirage. Then she'd generously expressed her delight in any and all good news I shared with a familiar "Well, that's wonderful!" Since those early years she has certainly grown used to her only daughter living three thousand miles away, but our relationship still relies on our ability to share more than just words via our voices over the phone.

Sometimes the news we shared wasn't wonderful, and the tension in her voice revealed pain or fear. When I appeared on *NYPD Blue* in the now famous, or perhaps infamous, shower scene I did with Sipowitz, she was understandably uncomfortable. Her reaction was complicated. She is inherently modest, so although the scene is touching and tasteful, her daughter's bare backside was still broadcast to the world. As much as she loved the show and was proud of my involvement, when we spoke on the phone after that episode aired, she wasn't critical but she didn't have much to say. I could hear the ambivalence in her voice and even in the breath she seemed to be holding. I certainly don't fault her, and even appreciate her restrained reaction.

We all seem to need our mothers when we are ailing, and my mom is a good nurse. Her instincts are solid and she is neither histrionic nor hovering. Before I moved to Los Angeles, I broke my nose in a waterskiing accident—don't ask—and required surgery to repair the cartilage. Hearing her gentle voice as I came around in the recovery room was so reassuring. And when I had to share the news of another health scare, hearing the heartbreak in her voice was perhaps the most difficult part of that journey. We aren't big criers in my family, so any crack of emotion in her voice feels like an earthquake to me.

As an actress, I use my voice for a living and am keenly attuned to vocal qualities. Because I live in a modern world and often communicate by emails and text messages, I am ambivalent about technology, which often robs me of the true emotions and connections I interpret through voices. But since my family lives so far away from me, I am ever more grateful for the miracle of wireless technology because I can reach Mom whenever I want: when I'm in the market and can't remember what kind of eggplants to buy for a ratatouille recipe she shared with me or to let her know Dad and I were safe on a cross-country road trip we recently made. And I appreciate how, like an aural album, digital storage allows me to hold the voices of those dear to me so they're just a keypad away—the voice mails of my eighty-four-year-old father-in-law singing his favorite song to me, my aunt with good news of her clear breast cancer checkup, my now deceased neighbor thanking me for the apple pie I baked him. These voices are precious to me and evoke both memories and profound gratitude because I can't see them but I can feel them; I can't hold them but they can stop me cold; I can't taste them but they nourish me; I can't duplicate them but I can save them forever.

Because I always pick up the phone when Mom calls, I don't

have any voice mails from her. I've got to do something about that. Someday her voice will be one of the only things I have left of her, but that sound, miraculously suspended in digital/ether, will continue to encourage, comfort, heal, and instruct how to better use my own voice.

Note to self:

The voice is the transmitter
of the heart's emotions.
Listen with care.

The Cosmic Shelf

BROOKE McMURRAY

Brooke McMurray is a former publishing industry executive and a passionate advocate for the sufferers and survivors of domestic violence. She has been a member of the board of directors of Safe Horizon, the nation's leading victim assistance organization, since 1996. As the national spokesperson for Safe Horizon, Ms. McMurray has been featured on *Good Morning America* and National Public Radio, and was the subject of a 2002 Lifetime Television special, *Fear No More: Stop Violence Against Women*. Before leaving the company in 2000, Ms. McMurray had a twenty-six-year career at Time Inc., where she held several executive positions related to the launch and marketing of more than thirty magazines. She is currently the president of World Benefactor, a company that develops online marketing solutions for nonprofits. Ms. McMurray resides with her husband in New York City.

Hi, Brooke? This is John F——."

"Huh. I used to go out with someone named John F——."

"You're talkin' to him."

Not a day went by without someone calling me up in hopes that I'd buy their services for my company. Being cold-called was part of my job. John F——was just another name. Until it wasn't.

It had been twenty-seven years since we'd seen each other. A generation's measure. He'd recently attended a high school reunion where an old friend had asked him about me. He learned I lived and worked in New York—he lived in a suburb nearby—and resolved to look me up.

We agreed to have lunch at Michael's—his choice—on West 55th Street. He was waiting for me at the table when I arrived: same bright, eager face, same big, heart-shaped smile he'd had when we were seventeen. *He looks younger than me*, I thought. I had the sense of having just seen him yesterday or last week, not a lifetime ago. We began by catching up about kids, jobs, that sort of thing. He realized, as most of the men I met did not, that my questions had two purposes: not only was I curious about him, but asking questions was a great way of not having to answer any. Quickly I found myself in an unfamiliar place: talking about me. Whoa.

He ordered a side of mayonnaise for his French fries—*heart attack food*, I thought. And yet there was something so unguarded, so *Midwestern* about his doing so. Like home. I hadn't thought of Ohio as home in twenty-five years.

When I got back to my office, my assistant was curious. "How'd it go?"

"Another unhappily married man who's not really aware of his unhappiness," I told her. Statement of fact.

A few days later at work, phone rings.

"You so captivated me that I left without paying the bill."

No intro. No "Hi, it's John." As if no time had passed since lunch. Since 1967 when we were seniors in high school.

I grew up in a small town near Cleveland; John grew up in Youngstown. Our fathers were well educated—mine at Harvard, his at Yale—and both had returned home to northeastern Ohio to live and work. Education was important to both families and we'd each wound up at private schools, me at day school near Cleveland and John at a boarding school not far away in Hudson. There, we had learned the same things, taught the same way. I was on the debate team, as was John's roommate. That's how we first met. My earliest memory of John is seeing him from a distance at a dance, schoolboy tweed jacket and tie firmly in place, dancing and singing along to—no kidding—"Johnny B. Goode" with confidence. With abandon.

We dated briefly in the spring of our senior year. I wasn't exactly Miss Popularity and felt fortunate to have a nice, fun, cute boyfriend to share that time with; weeks filled with parties and each other's proms and graduations—gentle rites of passage. We deciphered Sgt. Pepper's, danced to Major Lance, and smoked cigarettes in the car on the way to the drive-in.

Then it was off to college: me to Smith, and John, like his father before him, to Yale. I went to Yale only once, to a mixer. John met me at the bus; we went to his room, where we talked as if we were strangers. The evening ended early; back on the bus, back to Northampton, and . . . that was that. On to other things. Other fellas. Life. I never looked back once.

I married a man I met in college. As I've said about him in the countless speeches and articles I've given and written over the years: "My friends all said, boy, I bet your parents are pleased you married such a terrific guy." In fact, the marriage was a nightmare. My charming, well-liked, Dartmouth- and Stanford-educated, Morgan Stanley Associate husband belittled my friends and family, punished me for everything from bad weather to bad traffic to bad food, threw me out of a moving car, cut up every piece of clothing in my closet, beat me up at night, stalked me at work by day, and flaunted the Order of Protection I got from Family Court. And the whole time, I thought it was my fault. In those days domestic violence didn't even have a name.

Seven dark and stunting years later I finally got a divorce.

I fell in love with a man I met at work who was eighteen years older than me. First-generation Irish American. Devout Catholic. Quoted Yeats. Kept a list of his favorite songs—"What'll I Do?" comes to mind—scribbled on a matchbook in his jacket pocket. From him I learned the Great American Songbook and the pleasures of live music in small rooms. Bill. "Blythe Spirit," someone called him once. He had two adopted children—three really, but one of them had died in early childhood, and when he spoke about her it was like it had just happened.

Bill told me early on that his kids were adopted because he and his wife had been unable to have children of their own. And *that*, he quickly and gallantly explained, was due to *his* shortcoming. Surprised we were then when I got pregnant. Bill, not yet divorced, was overwhelmed with guilt. And me? I was thirty, unmarried, and miserable. I hated the idea of an abortion but doubted the alternative made any sense. So, I called my doctor and arranged to meet her at a clinic in the East 50s. She bustled in, iced coffee in hand, to find me sitting there crying.

"Look," she said. "We've got another week or so. Go home and think about it." So, we shared the coffee and talked.

A week later, I showed up at the appointed time, as did Dr. L, another coffee in hand. Still, I couldn't bring myself to go through with it. So, we split her coffee *again* and talked some more.

Another week, more uncertainty and another appointment. Dr. L had two coffees with her this time. "I'm spending a lot on cab fare here, and we're not getting anywhere," she said with gentleness and humor. "If we do this every week for nine months, you're gonna have a baby!" Exactly. Have a baby. Just saying it out loud, I knew it was right.

I made another appointment with Dr. L, but this time for my first prenatal visit.

Bill was of two minds about my decision. He didn't believe in divorce, and he didn't believe in abortion. As time went on, he became solicitous and supportive and *so* proud. He loved his children, but it mattered a lot to him that he was going to have a child of his very own. However, the guilt over leaving his family and marrying again never left him. I often thought it was what eventually made him sick.

We were married at City Hall two months after I made my decision, on Sadie Hawkins Day, 1980. I wore a red maternity dress with a white gardenia pinned to the collar. We lived in my little one-bedroom apartment near the UN and went to Lamaze classes together. I'd never been happier in my whole life. That August, the man who'd adopted children because he couldn't have any of his own watched as his son was born. Grey. "My Boy Gravity," Bill called him. "My fair son," Shakespeare said it best; "my life, my joy, my food, my all the world."

Seven years later, Bill died of cancer. I was thirty-seven and Grey not quite seven. Bill lived almost two and a half years from the time he was told he had but a few months to live, and for much of that time, he felt good. When he was first diagnosed, I grilled the doctors, asked a million questions, read everything about cancer I could get my hands on, even went to lectures at Sloan-Kettering meant for med students. Then I realized the details didn't matter; there simply was no cure. I was wasting time. *Just live.*

After he got sick, Bill wanted so much for life to be normal. "I'm *fine*," he'd say whenever anyone asked. His chemo nurse told me how unique he was. "We spend all our time trying to put our patients on a regimen that's convenient for *us*," she said. "I loved Bill because he fought endlessly to live his life his *own* way, to hell with the regimen." As the weeks and months passed, the man who couldn't bear to miss a party and was always the last to leave ("I'm afraid I'm gonna miss something," he'd explain) grew to love nothing better than sitting on the sofa at home after work, reading to Grey. "Together!" Grey would say as he put his arms around our necks and pulled our heads close to his.

"Grief," Anna Quindlen wrote in "Life and Death" (*New York Times*), "remains one of the few things that has the power to silence us . . . [It] is unspoken, publicly ignored except for those moments at the funeral that are over too quickly, or the conversations among the cognoscenti, those of us who recognize in one another a kindred chasm deep in the center of who we are."

"You don't have to get over it," my friend Paula, herself a widow at twenty-one, reassured me with kindness and understanding.

The fact that Grey was too young to completely understand

what had befallen us was the only saving grace. His buoyancy, his high jinks, his sweetness were like a salve.

"Is there anything good about Dad dying?" he asked one evening. His question threw me, and I had to think for a minute. *Well, yes,* I realized, *there was.* Those months and years of worrying about Bill were over. The nights of watching him breathe—and wondering when he would stop—were gone. At last I could give Grey the attention every little boy deserved. "I know why we try to keep the dead alive," Joan Didion wrote in *The Year of Magical Thinking.* "We try to keep them alive in order to keep them with us. I also know that if we are to live ourselves there comes a point at which we must relinquish the dead, let them go, keep them dead."

Little by little, I let go of Bill.

Friends and family reassured me: you'll meet someone else. And I did, but never the right someone. I had a therapist who called them all, with optimism and clarity, "the one before the One."

It took me a long time to figure out that finding the One wasn't just about being picked. It was about doing the right picking myself. "This month," my horoscope read in 1991 as I was finally beginning to see the light, "you may feel as though you are close to the answer and yet still far from your dream. Life seems to be a roller coaster at the moment. Every day tells a different story. Hints of change are all around you." Something about that gave me hope. I carry an almost unreadable copy of it around in my wallet to this day. A talisman.

Three years later, I heard from John.

Our pasts seemed uncannily intertwined; John lived in

Bronxville, on the same street Bill had lived before we were married. He had joined Bill's old golf club in the fall of the year Bill died. His older son's name, I learned, was Evan, the name of Bill's little girl who had died. And, like the children of Bill's first marriage, John's children were adopted.

John told me we'd been married, each for the first time, on the same day, at the same time: June 17, 1972, at 4:30 p.m., the day of the Watergate break-in. ("Oh, so you weren't the only person held up that day," a coworker had commented wryly to me.) John read my wedding announcement in the paper on the way to the airport for his honeymoon. I had the thought that we'd been stored on some cosmic shelf, saved for each other until some other, perfect time.

I realized quickly that while I'd been pretty much oblivious to the past all these years, John had kept the memory of me somewhere close. Inspired by his recollection that I rode horses as a child, he took up riding at thirty-five. And he returned regularly to the story of the day his mother wouldn't allow him to come visit me at a horse show because he had mono. As if that visit would somehow have changed the course of each of our lives.

He'd been married all those years to the same woman and held many different jobs. He had huge success by the time he was thirty, enormous wealth by forty-five. His was so unlike my own trajectory: one employer for twenty-two years—nearly my entire working life—two husbands, and too many Mr. Wrongs. Different paths, and both unsatisfactory, each in its own way.

And then, in a spate, his father died, he lost his job, and no one beat down his door to hire him like he'd imagined would happen. He claimed that "the barn wasn't burning" when I asked about his marriage, but he didn't act like a happy man. He showed me pictures of himself with his family; he was smiling in exactly none of them.

A few months after that first lunch, on a raw, early spring day, we had lunch again, this time with Tina, a mutual friend we'd known in high school. It was because of Tina that John had learned I lived in New York, and over lunch she asked John if he couldn't, please, be helpful and introduce me to someone. "What kind of man are you looking for?" she asked, turning to me.

"Nice," I said. "Just *nice*. Nice is what I'm looking for." It had taken me years, but finally, I realized nice was key.

John looked surprised. Later, he told me how he'd come to lunch imagining—without being aware of it—that he was there with me. My answering Tina had brought him up short. We were just friends. Period. We weren't together. And besides, he was married. What was he thinking?

We talked on the phone occasionally that spring, and something about those conversations was so comforting. How lovely to talk to someone my own age with so much shared history. I asked for his help with a business matter; he was trustworthy and eager to help. I found myself imagining what would have happened if I'd run into him earlier in life; could he have rescued me from my first marriage? Could he have prevented my grief?

I went out to Lake Powell in early July to meet an on-again, off-again boyfriend for a week on his houseboat. As I left, I told my assistant that I didn't care about any calls but to leave me a message if John F——called. *What was I thinking?*

And then, a few days later, at a phone booth on a dock at a red rock promontory called Dangling Rope, I heard her tell me he'd done just that. Yippee!

August. Grey was at his gramma's, where he'd spent every single summer of his childhood, three miles up a hill on a dirt road in New Hampshire. My boss was on vacation. John's family was "at the beach," wherever that was. So we agreed to meet for drinks after work one evening at the Polo Lounge at the West-bury. Usually prompt, I found him waiting for me: that guile-less face, that youthfulness. I never saw anyone so happy to see me. Ever. I sat down, aware that things had changed and this evening might turn out to be a big step. "I don't bite," he said, noticing how I'd crossed my arms defensively and twisted my legs, pretzel-like, around each other.

Drinks turned into dinner at a little place I went to often in my neighborhood. He had no idea where he was, and I realized he sure wasn't a New Yorker.

He kissed me on Madison Avenue as we left the bar. Sweet breath, dry, warm kiss—same as the kiss goodnight at Yale, as the kiss in the backyard at my friend's afterprom party, as the kiss in the park on a Sunday afternoon in Cleveland the week-end before graduation. Just like that, years dissolved.

That night at dinner, we began a conversation that has never stopped, not even once, since then. On through the evening it went, through the night (when had I ever stayed up *all* night long?), through breakfast. Everything was so quiet when he left. But unlike every other time in my life reminiscent of this one, I didn't wonder when or if I would see him again. I would; it was simply not possible that I wouldn't.

Restless, I called my old friend, Howard, and told him everything, like I always did. "Oh, my God, I'm going to be a bridesmaid!" he crowed. I laughed at that but I didn't disagree.

John called me when he stopped for gas on his way home, and I remember thinking that I wouldn't be able to take a shower and get to work if I couldn't get him to stop calling! I realized that, for the first time ever, someone liked me as much—in fact maybe even *more*—than I liked them. How about that?

He wasn't the first married man I'd fallen for, but I knew this was different. (Sure, my friends scoffed.) I'd learned by this time that if you felt you needed to ask where things were going, you already knew the answer: Nowhere. This time, there were none of those questions. A few months later, he packed up and left home for good.

Things did not go smoothly: his divorce took nearly forever, and his children and Grey might as well have come from different planets. He loved living in the suburbs, and New York was the only place on earth for me. Sometimes I thought about giving up. Lucky for me, John never did. He was determined and optimistic enough for both of us.

We were married five years after that first lunch, in the backyard of his big, fancy house with lots of friends and an eleven-piece band and my son strewing rose petals from a crinkled paper bag. My old friend Don, a lifelong poker player, was there.

"This is what I call drawing to an inside straight flush," he marveled.

I loved that. Yes, indeed.

Looking back, I keep thinking about the line from one of my

favorite childhood poems, "The Midnight Ride of Paul Revere."
At the end, when the story's been told, Longfellow writes:

> *You know the rest. In the books you have read,*
> *How the British regulars fired and fled,*
> *How the farmers gave them ball for ball*
> *From behind each fence and farmyard wall . . .*

Well, frankly, you know the rest of this story, too. It's the end of
every fairy tale you've ever read.

"I lost you once," John said before he left that first morning.
"Not gonna lose you again."

Note to self:

As Charles A. Beard said,
"When it is dark enough,
you can see the stars."

My Perfect Wife

ASHLEY PARKER

Ashley Parker is a journalist who works for the *New York Times*. She has also written for *Chicago Magazine*, *Glamour*, *The Huffington Post*, *Philadelphia Weekly*, and *The Washingtonian*. She lives in Washington, D.C.

Sooner or later, I ask every man I date if he'll be my wife.

I bring it up when our legs are wrapped together on a blanket in Dupont Circle, or when we're lying in his bed as he traces his fingers up my ribcage, or when we're walking through the city in early fall and the air smells like wet leaves and turns our cheeks a chilly pink. But the reaction is always the same: laughter, followed by confusion, followed by stammering protest as I soldier forward.

"Not my *wife* wife," I say helpfully, as if this distinction somehow matters. "But you know, *like* my wife. If we make it, that is. But would you be the one who stays home with the kids, and cooks dinner and cleans? Oh, and definitely the one who handles the bills. And grocery shopping—that is the *worst*. Did I tell you I almost had a panic attack in Safeway the other day?

I finally just grabbed a Gatorade and left. I know, doesn't bode well."

At this point, he is usually just staring at me, dumbfounded.

"Of course I'd work," I always continue. "I'd totally support us and work full time. While you were, you know, my wife."

It's not a feminist issue for me. My mom made the choice to stay home and raise my sister and me, and I know that being a wife means so much more than serving as the mother of all things cooking- and cleaning- and shopping-related. I also know I want to get married and have kids some day, and I'm sure I'll enjoy all sorts of domestic thrills. But I just can't summon the energy right now.

I've dated fantastic men—all of them—but no one has ever agreed to my wifely proposal. On the one hand, I totally understand. Even the most progressive men, the type who might one day agree to gender-neutral toys and proudly call themselves a stay-at-home dad, find my semi-joking leap to "wife" somewhat emasculating, a bit like if I'd suggested they grow some ovaries and carry our first child to term. But on the other hand, I can't accept anything less. I'm in a full-time relationship with my desire to write.

On my second day at my entry-level job as a research assistant at the *New York Times*, my boss tossed me the keys to her stick-shift Miata and I caught them with pride. I felt like a trophy wife, and the keys to her two-door, low-riding sports car were simply privileges that came with my role. This feeling lasted about five minutes, until just after I'd started the car—precariously perched on an incline—and went shooting backward down the ramp of our office parking garage, crunching to a stop just inches from a concrete wall. I eventually managed to jerkily creep out onto the street by keeping the parking brake engaged until I gunned the gas and lurched forward into drive. (Sorry, clutch.) It was terrifying and exhilarating all at once, and the challenge, responsibility, and promise of what lay ahead if I ever got out of the garage was a powerful combination.

I was an aspiring journalist and no task was too small for me. The Friday deadlines that stretched toward midnight? No problem. The late Tuesdays, when rolling out of work at 10:00 p.m. was considered "early"? I was happy to be there. The weekends spent researching obscure old movies or "organizing" the office (i.e., shuffling around huge boxes full of old Anita Hill/ Clarence Thomas files until the office looked not necessarily cleaner so much as a new and improved form of disorganized)? I was your girl.

I was also doing double duty—researching and fact checking by day, and playing reporter by night. Once I had a foot in the door at the *Times*, I wanted to prove myself as a journalist, so the remaining twelve hours when I wasn't officially at work I spent working as a de facto freelancer, making calls and reporting ideas and writing (and rewriting) stories.

As I focused on climbing the journalism ladder, relationships fell by the wayside. My boyfriend and I collapsed under the pressure of long-distance and post-college life. It didn't help that every time I went to visit him, our weekends in Philly would turn into the search for the perfect coffeeshop where I could get free WiFi.

"I'm so sorry," I would plead. "Just as soon as I track down this one expert on the history of Scandinavian misogyny, we can do something really romantic."

While my friends spent long brunches talking about the

medical residents they'd picked up at Capitol Hill happy hours who'd failed to call two days later, I talked about my editors with similar frustration.

"I sent him my story pitch three days ago—and not a word," I'd say. "And I'm not sure if I should follow up with him or what. I mean, I don't want to seem too desperate." If a book called *Your Editor's Just Not That into You* had existed, I'm sure my worried friends would have bought it for me along with a carton of Häagen-Dazs and staged an intervention.

Over Bloody Mary–fueled gossip sessions, my friends would gush about new clubs they'd discovered that were so Capital-C Cool that there was a secret door you had to know about. Not wanting to be outdone, I breathlessly revealed that I'd found a secret door to a shower just off a ladies' room in the *New York Times* office.

"So, you know, you can wash your hair if you get stuck late at work?" I offered, hopefully.

I had become like one of those Girls on the Rebound who could talk only about her ex, even on first dates with perfectly suitable guys. Except instead of a former lover, I babbled on about the adventures surrounding my boss's latest column or the newest political profile I was working on. When one guy I'd started seeing over the spring called me to say goodbye before he left D.C. for the summer, he told me about the mountains he was going to climb, and I told him about the pesky DNC spokesman who just wouldn't get back to me. I sent him a few emails while he was away, but when he returned after Labor Day, he never got back in touch and I didn't notice.

As my relationship with my job grew deeper and I began playing wife to my newspaper's fickle and ever-demanding husband, I started to feel like I was missing out on a crucial part of my twenties. I wanted to make up for lost time, and decided to jam all of my romantic "youthful indiscretions," as misbehaving politicians always put it, into one intense summer. I felt a bit like a newly divorced child-bride, eager to sample the world I'd missed as I was registering for dishes at IKEA and touring one-bedroom, one-baths with my too-serious fiancé. If I got all of this promiscuous folly out of my system crash-course style, I reasoned, I wouldn't have "missed" anything. I'd be able to commiserate with my friends ("I threw up all over his shoes and never heard back from him again," I imagined myself cheerfully recounting), and best of all, by autumn, I'd be ready to focus on my career again.

But my salacious summer quickly went bust when I discovered I couldn't even manage a proper one-night stand. The Yale junior (is twenty-four too young to be a cougar?) I clumsily picked up at Tryst—a coffeeshop where I was doing work on a Sunday, natch—put up a noble attempt, inviting me out for a night of what promised to be copious shots of cheap vodka. But by the time I met up with him late one Tuesday after I'd finally been sprung from work, we managed only a few-hour stand before I headed home to catch up on the next day's news. Sure, we still had all the telltale signs of a traditional one-nighter—cheap drinks, awkward conversation, a fumbling hookup, and the unspoken promise that we would never speak again. So I could officially check that off my list. But the whole time, in the back of my mind I felt like I was still on the clock, meticulously researching a story about a one-night stand rather than enjoying one.

When I first graduated from college wanting a career in journalism, I understood that long hours and nontraditional days were par for the course. That's part of what drew me to the field in the first place. But this was before I'd internalized the phrase "campaign nuns," which refers to the women who cover presidential campaigns. They are all talented, smart, funny, sexy, successful—and frequently single. Presumably, spending New Year's Eve in Des Moines, trekking around the country with just a carry-on suitcase and a sturdy pair of boots, and canceling dates at a moment's notice because Barack Obama just issued a breaking statement does did not endear you to potential suitors. (In our office, the gay men who didn't have children and thus had slightly more flexible schedules were also frequently found in the politics pod.)

In the D.C. bureau, we had a row of cubicles we jokingly called "Alimony Alley," because almost all of the reporters who sat there were recently divorced. Of the male reporters who were married, from what I could glean, their conjugal bliss was due in large part to their extraordinarily tolerant wives. One guy, when he had a big story due, would decamp to the office, working for days until the wee hours of the night when he would finally emerge, disheveled, from a cloud of papers, stacks of books, and rotting Cosí salads, then stumble home for a few hours of sleep long after any sane person would still be up. The toll the job put on people's personal lives was abundantly apparent, but this was the life that I desperately wanted; I loved writing and reporting, and I was willing to throw myself into it headfirst, even if it meant I might only ever be my newspaper's wife.

Finally it dawned on me that a fellow journalist might be more understanding of my plight. When I saw that we'd hired a cute grad student for the summer to help with the politics blog, I pounced. He's now my boyfriend, and a full-time journalist himself, but even he often jokes that he feels like he's in a relationship with me and my boss—a ménage à trois without the allure. In fact, our entire relationship could be measured in moments and milestones inextricably bound to my job. Our early "dates" took place at a Best Western in New Hampshire (one romantic evening was spent shoveling my rental car out of a snowbank), because that was the first place we were both present long enough to spend time together during the endless primary season. We have an unspoken understanding that plans are not to be made on deadline days or election nights or most Monday through Fridays. I think he puts up with the craziness—the dozens of weekends last year that I locked myself in coffeeshops by my house as I struggled to finish a feature story about young Obama aides for the *New York Times Sunday Magazine*; the time I left D.C. for a "quick trip" to L.A. with my boss and ended up missing his birthday—because he understands the rhythms of the industry. I've jokingly asked him to be my wife, and he's jokingly (I hope) said no way, but he does cook for me after long deadline days, TiVo the shows I like, and help brainstorm story ideas well into the night, and that's a good enough start.

When I was in L.A. missing my boyfriend's birthday, I ran into a girl I knew casually from high school. She'd been a journalist in D.C. for a while, but when I saw her, she was working at a clothing boutique in West Hollywood. Apparently she'd interviewed a musician over lunch one day, and when they'd finished he'd invited her to his show later that night. She went, they made out after his set, and a week later she was traveling with the band. She tried to find a journalism job when they moved to L.A. together, but nothing panned out, and besides, working retail gave her flexible hours so she could go on tour with her fiancé. Yes, they were engaged, and she glowed as she talked about her new and exciting life.

Every now and then I hear a story like this, about a girl and guy who meet cute, and then she pulls up stakes to go off with him, dashing into a whirlwind new life in Paris or London, New York or L.A. I love imagining myself in these stories—it all sounds so romantic, so spontaneous, so utterly Of the Moment—but I also know that this will never be my life. Though I've never specifically been asked to drop everything and follow some sexy, scruffy stranger to his villa in the South of France, I suspect our conversation would go something like this: "Sounds amazing— I'd love to go, but I can't this weekend. I'm working on a story and I have two interviews set up that I just can't reschedule, and next week isn't great because I'm getting back edits on my *Chicago Mag* freelance piece. But I may be heading over to London in May for a possible profile of this new author, so if you'll still be at your villa, I could maybe swing down for the holiday weekend. You do have wireless, right?"

I can picture the glazed eyes, the look of "You seem interesting enough but this just isn't for me," and I have enough self-awareness to realize that, try as I might, I will never be the type of person who drops everything, packs a suitcase, and takes a whimsical journey that might cause me to miss a story, or a possible job opportunity, or a call from a source.

So, for now, I'm happy to stumble along, knowing that my

boyfriend may not ever quite be my ideal of a wife, and I may not ever quite be his ideal of a girlfriend. But for us, this works. After all, as long as there's WiFi, there's always a chance for love.

Note to self:

**It's okay to be a wife
and want a wife of your own.**

Chronically Single

LIS PEERY

Lis Peery has been working in media and communications for over twenty-five years. Her first job out of college was taking personal ads over the phone at a free weekly in San Francisco. From there, she went on to help start a nonprofit that worked with homeless people, produce documentaries for cable TV, work as a film executive in Hollywood, write for a prize-winning neighborhood newspaper, and oversee the content of a booming website. Currently, Lis is developing a drama series for Scandinavian television and looking for her next adventure.

Technically speaking, I was single until I was forty-five years old. Aside from two relationships that lasted nine months each, a handful of grim blind dates, and countless drama-filled entanglements, I was someone who spent years at a time celibate, dateless, and utterly clueless as to why I couldn't find love. In fact, by the time I met my husband, Lachlan, I had resigned myself to the fact that I would probably be single until I died—and I still can't believe I'm married. As far as I'm concerned, it's a freaking miracle.

My first experience with the opposite sex was in first grade, when my best friend Sarah told me at recess that a cute, chubby kid named Peter Smith "liked" me and wanted to know if I liked him back. I looked around at my posse of first-grade girlfriends, all of whom had boyfriends by then, and knew that I needed one, too. I told Sarah yes, I liked Peter, and she walked over to him and his group of friends to tell them the good news. Our entire "relationship" lasted three weeks and was conducted by passing notes; Peter "broke up with me" by note, too. Next, a kid named Joe, who had a Justin Timberlake 'fro and was the most popular boy in the class, decided that he liked me, and we became boyfriend and girlfriend. After we'd been "dating" for three days, Joe inexplicably passed me a note and told me that I was going to be a slut when I grew up.

I had no idea what the word "slut" meant, and when I got home I asked my babysitter to look it up for me in the dictionary. When she read the definition to me I felt a deep sense of shame, though I couldn't have articulated why at the time. Joe had taken the liberty of predicting my future—a lonely, shameful future—without knowing me at all. How could he have the power to do that? Was it because he called himself my boyfriend for three days? We weren't friends, he didn't know me, and I had been handed over to him by a boy I had known only through notes. None of it made sense, but it made a powerful impression. After that, boys were officially a mysterious, vaguely adversarial territory that I navigated with nothing but confusion and a terrifying sense that surrender meant humiliation.

I'd like to say that my experiences with the opposite sex got better after first grade, but they never really did. The list of my inappropriate choices when it came to men is long and impressive in its diversity. There was Tony, a tiny Italian who was in "waste management" in Manhattan; then there was the guy I met at a basement party in the East Village and dated for three weeks before I realized he was a junkie; the guy whose dad killed his mom with an ax and who sobbed during sex; the writer who had a plastic mattress cover because he wet the bed; the cocaine-addicted guitarist who masturbated so much to internet porn that he couldn't have sex; the film sales agent with a tanning bed in his bedroom and a riding crop that he'd bought at Pierce Brosnan's yard sale; the Reiki healer who was ten years my junior and lived in a hotel . . . Many of them were wonderful, and some of them are still my good friends. But none of them were really boyfriend material, either because of a deficiency on their end or, ultimately, mine.

As the years passed and I tried again and again to date someone for longer than nine months, I kept finding that I never really felt like myself with anyone. Instead, I always felt like what I thought me-as-girlfriend would be, a composite of movies, books, songs, other women I'd seen be girlfriends, what I'd heard my male friends say they were seeking in their ideal mate. Never once did it occur to me that what someone might want to date was *me*, unvarnished and just as I would be to friends or loved ones. Instead, I started to feel as if mating and marriage were abilities that I hadn't been born with, a defect with which I'd have to live, like color blindness or bunions. As much as I wanted to find a man, fall in love, and settle into life with someone, I feared that something in me was too deeply flawed, or the right man for me was too elusive, for love ever to happen.

Because, let's face it, after a certain age, for some of us, being single can start to feel like having a chronic disease. Dinner parties, group vacations, and the holidays, most of which you attend solo, become minefields of self-pity and self-loathing: you negotiate them, but they can leave gaping wounds. Well-meaning people inevitably start to ask you why you're single ("I just don't get it. You're so great!), and set you up on blind dates with people you cannot fathom they might actually see you with. Women in relationships tend to eye you with distrust (are you going to steal their man?), and fellow single women compete with you for any heterosexual man within five miles. Loneliness is your stalker, but you can't get a restraining order.

Once your friends and family start getting married and having babies, the nightmare that is chronic singledom takes on an even more fevered pitch. An endless circuit of engagement parties, weddings, baby showers, and kids' birthdays begins, all of which you attend alone. It doesn't seem to matter how much money you make, how successful you are in your career, or how loved you are by your circle of family and friends; you cannot, for the life of you, figure out why you're single or how not to be. It's not like it's *always* awful being single. All you have to do is watch one of your friend's unhappy marriages up close to understand that in many ways you've dodged a bullet by not settling for someone who isn't right for you. Mostly, it's that you feel like you still haven't found the key that unlocks the door of your single girl prison, and that you could escape forever and never look back. But where is the damn key (others seem to find it so easily, or to have been born with it) and how in God's name are you going to find it? This is the question you ask yourself on lonely weekends, at the singles tables at weddings, as the only

single child left at family Christmases, at baby shower number
seventeen.

For me, finding the key meant that everything had to fall apart.

In quick succession, I lost my job in the film industry, de-
veloped a crippling case of "frozen shoulder" (which is exactly
what it sounds like), and watched my credit card debt and second mortgage do what so many other people's had done: come
howling at them like Hurricane Katrina. Within a matter of
three months, I was in financial, professional, and health crisis. I felt like I didn't even know who I was anymore.

Thankfully, just as I hit rock bottom, a friend recommended
her therapist. I contacted the shrink and quickly got to work on
myself. As I tried to get my arm working again, I dug as deeply
down into my battered psyche as I could and tried to figure out
how I'd ended up where I was at age forty-three. After a while,
my therapist's endless patience and my belief that I wasn't fundamentally wired for unhappiness helped me start to get to
know myself for the first time. My quirks, my faults, the things
about me that had been sabotaging my attempts at creating the
life I wanted were all dragged out into the light and examined.
Slowly, after pulling everything apart, I started putting myself
back together again.

As I learned more about who I really was and how I had come
to be that way, I could feel myself growing stronger. It was almost as if I were a tree in the forest, and each lesson, each moment of clarity I had, was a ring being added by the sun, wind,
and rain. At one point, I told my therapist, Elizabeth, that it
sometimes felt as if alchemy were taking place between us as

we worked; I could sense a power larger than her or me in the room. Some would say it was God, others would say it was the power of universal healing. All I know is that along with feeling as if I were going to survive—and hopefully thrive—I also lost my bitterness at being single. For the first time ever, I began to feel hope that someday I would meet a man I could fall in love with.

Somehow, I needed to translate this hope into action. I had been dabbling in online dating since my early forties—Match, etc.—and had found the experience to be a complete and total nightmare. I would post and click for six months, and then vow never to log on again. A few months later, I'd be back online as a gambler heads back to Vegas, thinking that *this* time I'd find a man who was actually who he said he was and who looked like his photograph.

Thanks to therapy, I was feeling stronger and more optimistic, so I decided to join the dating site PlentyOfFish.com. I liked the fact that it was free (eHarmony, which charges a fortune, sent me on a date with a stand-up comedian with five cats that still makes me question their "scientific approach" to matchmaking) and I liked the vibe of the site, which was friendly and no-nonsense.

My profile was short and sweet. It read:

> *Hello Clyde? It's Bonnie. I am a 45-year-old delighted to have made it this far! Life is good. Life is hard. Life is a wonderful adventure. I am fine on my own but have a feeling I'd be even happier with a man to share it all with. My interests are life, movies, adventures of any and all kinds, books, art, coffee, and my niece and nephew.*

Not long after I posted it, a note landed in my mailbox. It was from someone calling himself Scotsingle, and what he had to say about himself caught my attention:

> *Good man looking for a good woman! I'm a Scotsman looking for a woman to enjoy life with. I'm looking for someone who is nice and not too wild (a little wild is okay). I'm not a religious man and I don't have too many strong political views. I think, "Live and let live." I love animals and I enjoy staying in shape but am not obsessed with it. My interests are relaxing at home, going to concerts with my 18-year-old and 15-year-old, soccer, art, cooking, travel, movies, running, and music.*

What an unpretentious, nice profile! I thought. So I wrote him back.

I soon learned that Scotsingle's name was Lachlan. His photos showed a kind face with a strong chin and bright blue, twinkly eyes. We emailed each other for a while and he continued to come off as an honest and kind man. Eventually, I gave him my phone number.

The first time we spoke, Lachlan's Glaswegian accent was so thick I couldn't understand a word he was saying. Finally, after much laughing, spelling, and negotiating (he lived in San Clemente, which is an hour south of Los Angeles, where I lived at the time), we made a date to get together for coffee in Long Beach, which was halfway in between our respective towns.

Our date was set for 3:00 p.m. on a Saturday. After three years of sporadic online dating I tried to check my hope and excitement, but I couldn't help feeling it. I knocked on wood as I walked out the door, but three hours later I was hopelessly lost, sweating in my car (which had no air conditioning) and ready to turn around and go home. I had my cell phone glued to my ear and Lachlan was trying to give me directions as I drove, but due to his thick Glaswegian accent, I couldn't understand a word he was saying. (I found out later that I was being such a pain in the ass on the phone that he wanted to turn around and go home, too.)

Finally, after forty minutes of this, we ended up meeting at the Maritime Museum in the port of San Pedro, down the freeway and over a huge bridge from Long Beach, because it was the only landmark I could find. From there we walked to a restaurant called the Grinder, where Lachlan had last eaten twenty years ago. It turned out that his first job out of college had been fixing slot machines on cruise ships, and in those days they had docked in San Pedro. We talked later about the fact that, had I not gotten lost, he never would have gone back to the Grinder and revisited his very first days in America.

Lachlan always says that he fell in love with me the moment I took off my sunglasses; I fell in love with Lachlan about twenty minutes into our date. As I listened to him talk, and could actually understand his heavy accent because we were face-to-face, I also watched his strong, beautiful hands fiddle with his coffee cup and watched the love he has for his children move him to tears. I swear to God that in that moment, as I sat across from this man I had only just met, I felt my heart crack wide open, and warm, golden, syrupy light spread out across my chest.

Our first date lasted nine hours. We couldn't stop talking and kept walking around and around San Pedro, stopping every once in a while for another cup of coffee. I felt comfortable and happy to be with Lachlan, but what was even more striking was that I was being myself instead of my this-is-what-a-girl-friend-is self. The real Lis was walking around with this man, not one I was manufacturing to please him. It was a strange, invigorating feeling. Everything I learned about Lachlan drew me in more, too: he was honest, sweet, and funny; he loved his kids and had great taste in music; he drove a pickup truck and had a miniature Dachshund named Coco, whom he'd inherited when his ex-father-in-law died. When we had our first kiss, he said, "I can do better than that," and pulled me in for another one.

We met on August 31, 2008, and he proposed—at the Grinder—on March 22, 2009, just under seven months later. When we eloped on June 5, we had a celebratory dinner at the Grinder, where we were served by the same waitress who had served us on our first date and again when he proposed. She cried, and we have a photograph of the three of us together. Even on our wedding night, I still couldn't quite believe that I'd found a boyfriend, much less a husband. The whole process of being with Lachlan—of meeting, of falling in love, of being together, of getting married—has seemed so effortless that it has felt like a dream. Some kind of strange momentum kicked in the day we met and hasn't let up, which is the way it's supposed to feel, I guess.

Being married hasn't changed who I am, but it has changed how it feels to walk around in the world. I feel more settled inside, on a deep, almost molecular level. I feel myself leaning back into the knowledge that Lachlan is out there, loving me, at random moments of the day. As annoyed as I occasionally get with him, and he with me, I believe in the person he is and how he navigates the world. I still love looking at my wedding ring when I grip the steering wheel because it is a symbol of my connection to someone I love with all of my heart and soul. I never thought I'd write these words, but being married is healing something in my heart and in my soul every moment that I experience it. I trust Lachlan completely and, in turn, I love being trusted by him.

I wish I had the ultimate piece of advice for chronically single women who are searching for a partner like I was for so many years. I wish I could say what it was that changed in me, or the code I cracked inside that helped me find the key to what I regarded as the single girl's prison door. I know that I worked really hard on myself once I found out that my identity was built on sand, and that in retrospect my choices in men were not based on what my heart and soul wanted, but on what my impulsivity and recklessness wanted. I feel lucky that—ironically—my inability to be in a relationship meant that I was waiting for Lachlan, since I believe he is the man I was meant to be with all along. And I wish I hadn't been so hard on myself all those years I was single; I regret all the self-loathing I subjected myself to and the endless ways in which I compared myself to others.

What I did learn on my journey is that resilience and perseverance are essential, and that you shouldn't settle for less than you deserve. Humor and grace go a long way too, as well as the ability to be honest with yourself and with others about who you are and what you really need. I also believe that, in the end, sheer good fortune and a twist of fate might be the final answer to the question of love relationships. (On the one hand, this is completely unhelpful to those looking for love; on the other hand, it also means that love can happen to anyone.) After all, it was nearly four decades after my first-grade boyfriend wrote me a note predicting my romantic future that I received a note from Lachlan, but my luck finally came through.

Note to self:

**Don't settle for a partner
until you find yourself.**

Doing Just Fine

TAMEKA RAYMOND

Tameka Raymond, formerly a celebrity stylist, is best known for the trend-setting looks of Grammy Award–winning artists such as Lauryn Hill, Patti LaBelle, Jay-Z, and Usher. Her work has graced the cover of many well-known magazines, such as *Essence, Vogue,* and *GQ.* Currently, Tameka resides in Georgia and spends most of her time at her new boutiques, "Estella" and "Estella Home," and mentoring young girls through her Lost Ones Foundation. She is a proud mother of five amazing boys.

When I was a young girl growing up, I never fantasized about being married. While my friends were dreaming about their weddings and playing house, I was knee deep in the books, intent on becoming a lawyer or neurosurgeon. I was obsessed with increasing my vocabulary and fascinated by the human anatomy, and I could recite every muscle and bone in the body by the time I was ten years old. Meanwhile, my friends were busy practicing the signatures they'd use as future wives.

I knew that I wanted to have two kids, a boy and a girl; yet I didn't get so far as to imagine how I would have the two children without a husband (although I now know plenty of people do it). Primarily, I wanted to get a good education, become independent, and, ultimately, successful, and kids were part of that picture even though a marriage was not. Two marriages later, with a high-octane career as a celebrity stylist, a fairy-tale wedding and "Hollywood" divorce under my belt, and my own team of five boys, I realize now that life rarely turns out exactly the way we imagine it will, and love comes and goes just as haphazardly.

I grew up in a pretty traditional household in Oakland, California. My dad worked as a longshoreman and my mother was a stay-at-home mom. She chose to be at home while we were young so that she could hold down the fort and keep a close eye on my siblings and me. My parents were together for over twenty years, but they separated when I was a teen; I think I handled their breakup pretty well (this may have also had something to do with my views on marriage), and I learned to understand the concept of needing to move on.

By the time I was twenty, the lawyer/neurosurgeon dream had fallen by the wayside. Once I realized that you had to spend the better part of your life to become a success in either of those professions, I settled for my second passion: Fashion. I moved to Los Angeles and attended the Fashion Institute of Design and Merchandising (FIDM), where I majored in merchandise marketing and also learned the theory of sales and psychology behind the buying and selling of merchandise.

I got my big break into the world of styling, almost by accident, when a friend who was working with a record label asked me if I would do him a favor and help his new groups with their "look." I figured, why not, and threw myself into the project.

The task was a good fit for my "never-take-no-for-an-answer" attitude, and that first styling job led to another and another. Soon I was on my way to an exciting new career, learning as I went along. At first I charged next to nothing for my services, which probably helped me to secure a lot of clients in the beginning. However, over the years, as I grew to understand my worth and the going rates, it became easy to travel, make a great living, and enjoy myself while doing so.

When I first met Usher, I was juggling a thriving career, styling artists such as Patti LaBelle, Jay-Z, Toni Braxton, and Lauryn Hill alongside my other busy job: being a wife and a mother to my three sons. At the time, I was married to my high school sweetheart, whom I'd known since I was fifteen. We were in love for a long time, but over the years we'd become somewhat distant and more like brother and sister than husband and wife. We were still very close friends, and excellent parents to our kids, but we both knew that our marriage was in serious trouble. I believe that my career also played a role in our growing apart; I was constantly traveling for work, and like so many women today, I wanted to have it all, though it turned out to be much harder than it sounded.

In the middle of this balancing act, I was hired in August 2001 to image-consult and style Usher for his music videos and press tour for his album *8701*. Pretty much everything he wore in public after his first video and during the promotion for the record I put together for him. When we first met, it certainly wasn't love at first sight. In fact, it was barely like at first sight. I felt he was extremely hard to work for. His attention to detail is like no one I've ever met, and he has the memory of an elephant. I've found that when you work for someone like that, there's always this fear that you're going to screw something up, so in the beginning you're constantly walking on eggshells, until you learn what actually works and what doesn't. Once we got past that phase, we ended up discovering that we shared the same zeal for fashion; not just the final product, but the fabrics, their origin, the manufacturing details—all of it. Making that connection helped our professional relationship go much more smoothly.

In 2006, five years after I first started working for Usher, our relationship started to change from just business to a spark of something more, and then a crush that blossomed into love. He had gone through a breakup, and my husband and I were separated and going through a divorce. We were spending a lot of time with each other on the road, shopping, eating, and sometimes just simply talking. He would ask my advice about women and I would ask him about men and we would compare notes trying to figure out how the other sex operates and thinks. It was during those long talks that I started to see the side of him that's more than his stage presence, more than his voice, more than just the artist. I'd like to think that I saw a side of him that no one else had ever seen. I began to fall in love. I fell for his creative yet simplistic ways, old-fashioned spirit, and his passion for his artistry; he's a very serious person when he's not performing, much different than many people saw him, and we were very much of one accord.

When we first became romantically involved, we kept it pretty quiet. We dated for about one year, and there were a lot of ups and downs in our relationship due to our schedules and "outside" influences. While our dating was a secret to the outside world, it wasn't to close friends and family. I was separated and going through my divorce, and neither one of us was ready to announce the relationship, much less get married. In fact, I don't think we had ever discussed marriage.

So, in January 2007, when he proposed to me in front of his close friends and colleagues, I couldn't believe my eyes or ears. We were in New York to attend one of his best friends' daughter's christening, and afterward had gone to the studio to work on some music for his upcoming album. There we were, with this big group of people, including the incredibly talented musician Robin Thicke, with whom he was working at the time, when suddenly he said: "I'd like to make an announcement." I thought he was going to make some sort of declaration about his music or career in general. He called in the sound engineer, his security guard, assistant, and road manager as Robin played around on the keys, playing "Stupid Things." Then Usher began singing the lyrics, "All the stupid things I do have absolutely no reflection on/How I feel about you."

Then he really went for it. He said, "You guys all know how I feel about this woman. I love her more than I can express. We go through our ups and downs, our ins and outs, but I absolutely love her." He turned to me and continued, "I want to be with you forever."

I felt as if my face was on fire. I was so nervous and embarrassed, I was praying for his little announcement to be over quickly. He then said, "Wait a minute . . ." and started running around as if he'd lost something, and we all thought it might have been his mind for a minute there. He disappeared briefly, and when he came back into the room, he bowed in front of me as he slipped a little piece of yellow yarn onto my finger. As I stood there completely amazed, he said, "I'm going to replace this soon, but will you marry me?"

The world stood still; I will never forget that beautiful moment. Robin let out a little funny screech and started to play some piano riffs as I burst into tears and said, "*Yes!*" I would have gotten married that minute. I was a far cry from the little girl who had opted for thesauruses and anatomy books over marriage fantasies.

We kept our engagement private for about a month (and on Valentine's Day, as promised, he replaced the little yellow string with a gorgeous ten-carat Asscher cut diamond ring). With the exception of a few family and friends, we didn't tell a soul. After working with and being around famous people for so many years, we knew that it was likely that any news story about a relationship would quickly turn into something negative and ugly, and Usher and I already had a few strikes against us: our age difference (he's seven and a half years younger than me); the matter of my divorce not being finalized; and the fact that he's a superstar who had become famous as a teen, and his fans felt like they had a stake in his happiness, his career, and life choices, thus his viability as an artist. I wasn't prepared for the media scrutiny, and I certainly wasn't prepared for the onslaught of negativity that would soon come our way.

Despite our industry/experience, our secret soon became very public. We went to the NAACP Theatre Image Awards, where he was to accept an award for his work as Billy Flynn on Broadway in the musical *Chicago*. When we got there, he was beaming, and began telling people that we were engaged and how excited he was. Even more, when he got up on stage to accept his award, he said, "I'd like to thank my mother, everyone from the Ambassador Theater, and my fiancée for all the tireless hours she stayed up rehearsing with me." The room was stunned. I felt like all the eyes on me were burning a hole in the back of my head as I just sat there with a smile plastered on my face.

It wasn't that I didn't want the world to know. I just wanted the innocence and beauty of our engagement to last a little longer. Nevertheless, with that announcement, our privacy flew out the window. All of a sudden the media, the naysayers, the bloggers, and all the gossipmongers started talking shit and creating scenarios. I was painted as this much older, gold-digging woman who wanted to control Usher's career. They also latched on to the fact that I was still legally married, which taken at face value doesn't sound so great. But the truth was that my first husband and I hadn't lived together for a couple of years at that point, and we were legally separated. Due to the fact that we had children, the divorce settlement took longer to finalize (the courts don't let you out of your legal agreement as easily when there are kids involved). Yet, of course, all the press would report was that I was still married.

We managed to weather the scrutiny, but after Usher and I got engaged, he began to make many changes in his life. One of the most notable was replacing his manager, who also happened to be his mother. That was when the shit hit the fan. Basically, he had risen to fame in the industry as a teenager and had always been very close to his mother; she went with him to award shows, and he was the kind of son who always "thanked his mama." So I was blamed for their split, when in fact his decision had been previously analyzed and had nothing at all to do with me. It really didn't look good for either of us. Another major factor was my noncelebrity status. His first public girl-friend and the first one his fans really came to know had been a celebrity, so the public gravitated to her more readily because she was well known as part of a multiplatinum singing group in the nineties. It's weird how that makes a difference, but it truly did and does. I often got blamed for their break up.

In the subsequent months after our wedding I felt like I got blamed for everything that happened to him, whether it was weight gain, a bad hair day, or a bad jacket. The media attacked me constantly, and sometimes I would respond, feeling the need to defend myself or my marriage, only to make matters worse. I learned that the media, bloggers, and armchair analysts had a much larger, louder, and far-reaching voice than I had as an individual. The negative and nonsensical voices outnumbered me, and the people who were supportive generally did not com-ment publicly. The bloggers and those who left comments were vicious; I was referred to by some as old, fat, crazy, a cougar, a gold digger, even a tranny. But the most hurtful thing of all was that people suggested I would leave my kids from my previous marriage to chase a superstar. That whole notion is so ridicu-lous and insulting. Nothing could be further from the truth. My sons take precedence over everything in my life.

Ultimately, I'm a big girl and mature enough to know that words are only hurtful when you attach meaning to them, so I tried to remain as oblivious as I could and not read too much into them. Yet I'm only human. I still don't quite understand why there was such hatred out there for me, my relationship, his love for me, and for the love we shared, and I don't know if I ever will.

On top of the media's criticism, I started to lose trust in him. He had a track record of being a ladies' man and there was always constant temptation—and I felt it.

So there we were. The world, it seemed, disapproved of our marriage. Usher became unsure about his decision to marry me. I became insecure about everything. The album he recorded that was basically an ode to our relationship sold only a little over a million copies, which is a huge blow to an artist who is used to selling ten times that amount. Usher has always had an allegiance to his fans, and when they send a clear message like "I don't like your wife," it's hard, maybe even impossible, to overcome that.

A few months after our second son, Naviyd, was born in December 2008, things started to take a turn between us. Our ability to communicate with each other changed and his loyalty was in question. It soon became clear that the only thing to do was to part ways. So about nine months after the album came out, nearly two years of marriage and two beautiful sons later, he decided that he wanted to split. I don't blame him for the divorce entirely; I just wish the dissolution of our marriage was primarily due to internal factors as opposed to external. Unfortunately, the love that we had for each other, our commitment, and our family simply couldn't weather the storm. I think it is virtually impossible for any young couple to survive what we went through. In hindsight, I realize that we did more in one year as newlyweds—buying a house, releasing an album, traveling the world, having a baby, getting a dog, and simply learning to efficiently coexist—than many couples do in a ten-year span, and given all of the strain we were under from various fronts, I'm proud of what we accomplished together.

These days, I try to let the love that I have for life, my children, as well as my goals, carry me forward relentlessly. I have my five gorgeous boys; two retail boutiques named "Estella"; Kangazoom, an indoor children's facility; and I'm working on a private-label clothing line. I trust and have faith in God, and I believe that He has a greater plan and that all of this was part of my journey toward whatever is yet to come. I am confident that my humble beginnings, hard work, career successes, and challenging marriage have all made me a stronger, more resilient woman, who is optimistic about what her future holds. While I may not have a degree in law or a PhD in neurology, I think the younger version of myself would say that I'm doing just fine.

Note to self:

In terms of complexity,
human anatomy has nothing on
the anatomy of a relationship.

The Correction

ANNE K. REAM

Anne Ream is a Chicago-based writer whose work has appeared in the *Los Angeles Times,* the *Chicago Tribune,* the *Atlanta Journal-Constitution,* and numerous other publications. A past finalist for the Dorothea Lange–Paul Taylor Documentary Prize for her stories of women who have lived through violence and abuse, she is the founder of The Voices and Faces Project, an award-winning documentary project, and also the cofounder of Girl360.net, a Webzine for tween and teen girls. Her mother loves this essay (yes, really).

I was born to parents who had a tenuous hold on marital love in fact, if not in appearance. Our family life glimmered nicely enough on the surface—doesn't it usually, when enough energy is invested in appearances?—but behind closed doors my father was the Great Santini of the Chicago suburbs, demanding much, darkening quickly, retreating into his basement office and brooding in the glow of his fish tanks every time my brother's high school baseball team, or the Chicago Cubs, lost a game (this made for quite a lot of brooding). He had been the only child of two parents who adored and indulged him in equal measure, and—having spent his first twenty-two years at a series of "good schools" punctuated by idyllic summers made up of fly-fishing, canoeing, and rather obsessive bird-watching—he graduated college, met my mother, and became engaged to her not long after. I imagine that he settled into married life with not so much a thud as a shudder. Consumed with longing for the freedoms he had known growing up, and weighed down by the responsibilities of a wife and, in short order, three children, my father's life was not so much chosen as imposed. He was young, nervous, horrible at small talk, disgusted by convention and the bourgeois, and by turns indifferent to—then vicariously invested in—the successes of his children. Never was a man less suited to collegial life in the suburbs.

My mother was pretty and kind—always kind, too kind—and she knew how to make the best of things, a quality that has been many a woman's undoing. At the end of the year, her children's achievements ("Kary is a cheerleader! Bobby was on homecoming court! Anne made the varsity tennis team!") were breathlessly recounted in the Ream family holiday letter. No one wrote a better holiday letter than my mother. Every word she wrote was true—she was scrupulously honest—but somehow the story itself always seemed to be a lie. Sure, the three of us were smart enough, eager enough to please, but it was desperation, not ambition, that drove us. We knew the secret to our parents' happiness, and we were it.

Growing up, I was not so much my mother's daughter as her observer, my mind a hidden camera recording what I saw and storing it away until I could make sense of her choices. I patterned myself in opposition to her. My mom was a dreamer, in the saddest sense of the word: she believed in her dreamscape long after it was dotted with the dark clouds of my father's mounting frustrations with suburban life. Still, if it often felt like "The Reams" were a mirror held up to her lovingly constructed idea of a family, even I had to admit that the reflection sometimes had the power of the real. When, years later, my mother finally left my father, we were genuinely sad. Who would we be without her familial story line to guide us?

This is the baggage I carried as I raced out of my home and onto a Midwestern college campus. I loved tennis, wrote bad poetry, and drank quarter beers. I did not consider myself pretty, but I seemed to be pretty enough. I hadn't an ounce of ego to spare. I obsessed over rock 'n roll and hero-worshipped David Bowie. You couldn't go anywhere that fall without hearing a track from his *Let's Dance* album, but it was "Ziggy Stardust" that I played at maximum volume, exactly as directed. "Rock and Roll Suicide" was the song I loved best. It was its bravado, not its sadness, that moved me. "You're wonderful!" I'd sing along, like a mantra, willing the words to be my own words, and true.

I may have patterned myself in opposition to my mother but my radical girl chic was more interior than facade. How else to explain the fact that I pledged a sorority known for its bland, blond, and frequently wealthy Midwestern "sisters"? I was neither blond nor wealthy nor, I like to think, bland, but no matter: I was now one of them. This was a position that seemed to suit me—at the age of eighteen, I preferred to wage my rebellions from inside, not outside, the dollhouse. In the big white mansion on Nevada Street I found myself surrounded by, and at times genuinely fond of, girls who seemed to have been adored all of their lives. I learned how to approximate the subtle gestures that told the world that I, too, had been so loved, but the effort felt forced, and as dishonest as it was. When my roommate's father came to visit during a parents' weekend, I listened to the way that she said "Daddy"—proprietary and assertive, more a command than a name—and I envied her that a little. But I knew even then that I had something that most other girls did not. What it was, I could not articulate, but that mysterious thing was inarguably there. And so my envy never went too deep.

Some animal instinct warned me to avoid the dangerous boys, the ones who might tell you that they loved you but weren't, in the end, very loving. I couldn't risk anyone who seemed even vaguely unresolved, as my mother, in a fit of confidence, once told me my father had seemed to be. At twenty-one, I had had three love affairs of note—two in high school, one in college—but they functioned largely as wallpaper: a necessary backdrop to this girl's high school and college life, never front and center in my psyche.

And then, at the end of my junior year in college, I met Cliff.

He was seated next to me at a college dinner honoring "student leaders of exceptional achievement," a dinner he would have been invited to without question, but one I had likely squeaked into by a hair and a bit of extracurricular charm. I had known of him for a long time—he was a protégé of fiction writer Mark Costello, our campus literary star, and he had racked up a long list of awards and accomplishments. Sitting next to Cliff, I felt something I had never felt before: the shock of the familiar. There was no logical reason for this, because on the surface we had little in common. He was handsome in a Ted Hughes if only Ted Hughes had showered sort of way: dark and tall and rather brooding, bothering little if at all with the small talk I had been raised to believe was "good form." Our dinner that night was held in a cacophonous campus dining hall, where one hears the sounds of a crowd but no easily discernable words, and I remember that I had to lean in to listen to him over the din of the table conversation. The effort was worth it.

He had a reputation for a difficult-to-pigeonhole decency. He rarely missed mass; on quiet Sunday mornings, when the campus was collectively hungover (and he, no teetotaler himself, was likely hungover as well), Cliff was reliably one of the few students in the pews. However reckless he might have been the night before—and I had seen him out and suspected that he might have the capacity for real recklessness—he was properly penitent the next day. This I found deeply reassuring and oddly sexy. His Catholicism came to seem rather seductive on another level: I come from a long line of reliably anti-papist WASPs, and that faint whiff of familial prejudice lent the beginnings of our relationship a Montagues and Capulets style allure, defiance being the great aphrodisiac of the young.

From the start we clicked over a series of opinions, almost always about music and books. Was the Clash a better band than the Ramones? Who was to blame for the fact that the Police, after two great, raw albums, had become so overproduced? How did Sharon Olds manage the neat trick of writing poetry that was simultaneously overwrought and deeply moving? Was *The House of Mirth* a feminist cautionary tale or a reactionary argument for marriage? Did you have to be a fool, or just an ideologue, to actually believe that *The Fountainhead* had literary merit? *Tender Is the Night* or *Gatsby*? Fitzgerald or Hemingway? The Stones or the Kinks?

The words themselves didn't much matter. *You will never be bored with me* was the subtext of our conversations, and, amazingly, we weren't. We drank cheap wine, talked late into the night, and fell asleep with our limbs intertwined, often mid-sentence. On late afternoons we sometimes lay in bed with our books—he was then an aspiring writer who lived in books, and I liked nothing more than discovering a new title in his already enviable library. We read for hours, punctuating the silence by reading out loud a passage that was either very beautiful or very bad.

Mostly, we plotted our shared future, because both of us were serious, and seriously ambitious, eager to put so much distance between ourselves and our limited and limiting suburban upbringings that our familial antecedents would come to matter not at all. Cliff introduced me to Mott the Hoople's "I Wish I Was Your Mother," and the lyrics—"I wish I was your mother, I wish I'd been your father, and then I would have seen you, would have been you as a child"—captured perfectly an impossible, shared desire: to know one another in the past the way we were coming to know one another in the present.

It was the image of Cliff, and not the actuality, that shocked me into realizing that I loved him. Not long after we became a couple, he had mentioned (rather casually, as was his way) that he volunteered for the Special Olympics. And one day I picked up the campus paper and looked at a cover photo of an exuberant young girl—she could not have been more than eight or nine—leaning into the camera as someone placed a Special Olympics medal around her neck. And I knew, as I looked at the barely visible back of the head of the person doing those honors, that it was Cliff. His physical person had become so familiar to me, was so examined by me, that I could identify him by an eighth of an inch wide sliver of a photo. I was beginning to know him.

We left the Midwest, he for graduate school, first in the United Kingdom and then in New Haven, Connecticut; me for my first "real" job in Washington, D.C., at a grassroots lobbying and communications firm. Taking turns making the weekend drive between D.C. and New Haven never felt like a burden: the commute was a totem to our crazy-happy devotion to each other. Mostly, I came to appreciate that long drive because at its end Cliff would be waiting for me outside his lousy little graduate student apartment, situated eerily above a funeral parlor, and the weekend conversation would begin.

What seems touching now, from the standpoint of age and relative privilege, is how little we had, how little we had yet made of ourselves, and how utterly irrelevant that was to the question of happiness. Nostalgia, of course, is the tenderest trap, and those days have taken on a hagiographic glow. But the happiness, even under examination, holds up. My religion at that time was our future, and I believed in it with all my heart.

It is odd, in retrospect, how ordinary the events are leading up to an extraordinary shift. One looks back on the days or weeks that precede a traumatic event, stunned that somehow the menace did not make its coming known. But the weekend before I was the victim of a kidnapping and rape was a benign and happy one. It was Thanksgiving, and Cliff and I had decided to forgo the traditional trappings and make vegetarian burritos with a group of friends. I remember that after our dinner,

Cliff's classmate Curt, who was insufficiently vain and graduate school cheap, asked if I would cut his hair. Disregarding Cliff's warnings—"I'm in love with her and even I don't trust her with my hair"—Curt subjected himself to my styling ministrations (he would pay for his lack of vanity for months to come). I can still remember laughing at that bad haircut, perhaps because it would be a long while before I could laugh like that again.

It is difficult to describe the "before and after" that occurs when one has lived through the violent. One day you are a woman coming home from the grocery store the Monday after a Thanksgiving holiday, a member of the community of the ordinary. The next, you are in a hospital, your body a crime scene, the hours before a blur because they must be; immediately recalling what you had gone through would be almost too painful to bear. In the emergency room of Georgetown Memorial Hospital I remember having two distinct and powerful feelings. One was sheer joy that, however altered I might be, I was still alive: I knew without an ounce of doubt that I would come back from this, different but no less vital. The other, stronger feeling was impatience: I could not wait for Cliff, who had been called and was driving through the night, to get there.

He arrived in the early morning, stayed by my side until I could leave the hospital, and held his arm around me tightly as we walked into the bright light of an improbably perfect autumn day—so perfect that it felt like a cruel joke—and in that moment the violence that had been visited on me the night before became real. "Is this a joke? Is my life a joke? Is God laughing at me?" I cried out in the car as we sat in the hospital parking lot, and in that moment, as Cliff stroked my hair and I wept, I finally knew what it meant to be truly intimate with another person.

Despite entreaties from my family to leave Washington, I refused to quit my job or head home. It seemed to me then that a retreat might be the beginning of a collapse—that if I gave up any one aspect of my life, its entire architecture might come crashing down, never to be rebuilt. This was where I discovered that I was more my mother's daughter than I had thought: putting on a serene public face was an effort, but one that I was fully capable of. My mother's gift—constructing a narrative that assured the world that all was good and well—became my own. I imagined a woman who had lived through violence and emerged triumphant, and willed myself to become her.

In a sense, I existed in two worlds. There was my private life with Cliff, where I unleashed my hurt and fear and every last detail of being kidnapped and raped. And there was my public life, where I lived, as much as possible, as if such a thing had never occurred at all. One, over time, would become the casualty of the other. But for years Cliff bore the burden of my private sadness so gracefully, and so stoically, that I came to convince myself that I was not burdening him at all. When he published an award-winning short story based loosely on the facts of that evening—a gorgeous bit of testimonial fiction that captured the complex ways that terror and love can come to coexist—it reinforced my belief that violence could be turned into both art and incentive. I was certain that together we could create a life so unbreakable that one awful night years earlier need be only a tiny bump in our biographical road.

This was true for a time—well over a decade, actually. We moved back to Chicago, where I renovated a downtown loft and we pursued a complementary set of careers (His: writer and literary critic. Hers: advertising creative director). Serious animal lovers, we acquired a much-loved cocker spaniel, Baxter. I listened closely to my single friends and colleagues—a community of the young and often fabulous—and their stories reinforced what I had long felt: that the thing that Cliff and I had was unusual, perhaps even enviable. We were a country of two.

Still, having found my mother's too-early coupling horribly retro, I could not avoid the nagging feeling that I was now acting out a more contemporary version of her story. My girlfriends didn't just have partners, they had romantic portfolios, investing and divesting themselves of interesting men and women at a breakneck pace. At dinners and lunches they brought to the table a series of headlines; I, monogamous since I was twenty-two, had only a long story, the same story, one in which too many of its chapters seemed to be a study in seriousness.

Ambition was, for me, a talisman against history. Superstitiously, I believed that if I could become the things that someone who had lived through violence was never expected to be, it might begin to feel as if the past had not happened at all. Such ambition comes at a cost: Cliff and I were often separated by distance and professional space, the solitary life of a writer being sharply at odds with the commercial life of an advertising creative director. Yet so sure were we of our own solidity that serious attempts to navigate such differences were never even in the offing. Naïveté being the glimmer twin of hubris, we foolishly believed that the language of compromise was for other, lesser pairs.

We wrestled with more mundane issues as well. He disliked the Midwest and wanted to relocate to Paris to work on his languages and write; I was sure that if I asked for such a transfer, I would be bounced off my advertising fast track and never welcomed back on. And then there was the looming, nagging question of marriage, something we always agreed that we wanted "someday," albeit in a form very different than what we had observed growing up. Yet despite—or was it because of?—the increasingly vocal entreaties of our families to "settle down," "someday" did not seem forthcoming.

All of this might have been surmountable if our relationship existed only in the now. But over time, our shared past—the one in which Cliff had known the most broken parts of me—came to feel like a reproach to my carefully constructed present. His intimate knowledge made my history of violence real. Slowly, then powerfully, I wanted to escape such knowledge, and at times I suspected that he wanted to escape it, too. Perhaps our relationship cracked under the weight of its own seriousness; perhaps it broke finally because it should have broken years ago. In the end, the essential problem was this: our shared memories, wonderful and terrible, had come to feel like a restraint, not a bond. Fifteen years after we'd met, our relationship ended.

After we parted, I grieved for Cliff in a series of almost ritualistic ways. I shrunk my social circle to include only those I most trusted, traveled with my brother to London to "start again," refused to drink so much as a glass of wine—imagining that it was important to fully feel my loss at every moment—and eschewed all romantic encounters. "You've got to get out of this slump, Anne," one of my notably pre-feminist friends advised during my twelfth month of celibacy. "Really! Think of it this way: you're still young enough to be a trophy wife, and now you've actually done enough to have a few trophies of your own." Well, thanks—I guess.

My friend Paul was more appropriately encouraging: "You get ten years off for loving rock 'n' roll! That means you're really still, like, twenty-five," he declared by way of a pep talk. It was true that the late eighties—when I had last been single—were over and I now had smaller hair and much better shoes.

I finally was a woman with a bit of ego to spare. I coproduced an indie rock benefit album, and founded a nonprofit documentary project that racked up a bit of press and even a few awards. I had begun to love my work with the intensity once reserved for my personal life. And then, sixteen months after Cliff and I had parted, I was ready to try again.

Matthew was a former colleague who had left his advertising career to become an actor and, as goes with that poorly paid territory, an occasional model. We had known each other for years. I liked and trusted him in equal measure, and he—Second City–trained and seriously funny—knew how to make me laugh. One night, I accompanied him to a downtown party hosted by his modeling agency. As we made our way to the front bar, he turned to ask me what I wanted to drink, touching the small of my back, and in a cavernous loft full of beautiful people, I became—or felt like—the most beautiful girl in the room. It was the first time in a very long while that I had felt the shimmer of real desire. Faster than Screamin' Jay Hawkins could sing "I Put a Spell on You," Matthew had.

We were together for two years, and he was lovely in almost every way—except for the fact that He Was Not Cliff. My feelings for Matthew were real, even intense, but there was nowhere for us to go. After Matthew, I spent several years dating a Capitol Hill economist who was working for a rising political star with serious presidential aspirations. He was young, clever, and am-

220 LIVE AND LET LOVE

bitious, yet surprisingly and sweetly grounded. This was a man
who should have been exactly right for me—except, after a time,
I realized that I didn't want him to be.

Finally facing up to my own emotional limitations, my dating life evolved into something new entirely: a series of inter-
actions always predicated on someone else's desire, never my
own. I might meet a man, he might ask me out, and if I were
bored, or lonely, or wanted a date for an event, I might say yes.
It was all not so much tawdry as trite: ephemeral and light as air,
leaving the faint chill that essentially vapid relationships, even
of the several months long variety, often leave. I was racking up
the sort of romantic biography I had once admired in my far
more worldly friends. So why was I so bored? Why was I drinking so many martinis? Why couldn't I stand myself with any of
these men? Was this all that there was?

Some sort of denouement came in the form of yet another
economist, an assistant professor at a school famous for its lib-
ertarian and conservative bent. We met in a book group, dis-
agreeing over *The Confederacy of Dunces*—he liked it, I didn't,
which a more prophetically inclined mind than my own might
have seen as a harbinger of things to come. He could be charming, and for a while we had great fun, but he relished the role of
the deliberate contrarian (contrarians of the accidental variety
have always been far more compelling to me), and our world-
views diverged sharply. Noting that a bio he had read referred
to me as an "activist" on women's issues, he declared himself
a "pacivist," carefully spelling the word so that I was certain to
get the joke.

When a girlfriend invited me to a fund-raiser for World Bicycle Relief, a nonprofit organization that she had cofounded

that delivers bicycles—and thus transport—to health care and aid workers in war-torn and impoverished countries, he came as my date. There, over the din of the gathering and after two glasses of wine, he leaned in and mentioned that at lunch that day, he had been discussing World Bicycle Relief with his academic colleagues. "We all agreed," he said with a laugh that veered troublingly close to a sniff, "that bicycles certainly don't need any relief."

And in that moment, unbidden and unwanted, an image floated up: there was Cliff, in that long-ago newspaper photo, placing a medal on the chest of that little girl who had won the Special Olympics. An activist, in the best and loveliest sense of the word, to the core.

The realization came down, swift and hard: I did not belong here, the "here" not being in the presence of any specific man, but away from the one man who existed for me at the intersection of the ideal and the real. I had never really stopped missing Cliff: his essential kindness, his easy brilliance, his gorgeous writing, his great love of dogs. But the thing I most missed was the very thing I had been so frantic to flee: the feeling of being known by him, and the feeling that I actually liked the me that he had known.

It had been a long time since I had liked myself with, or even fundamentally revealed myself to, a man. Just as surely as I had done a passable imitation of a sorority princess all those years ago, I was now playing the part of a dating sophisticate. The effort, once frothy and fun, had now become forced and artificial and purposeless, not so much a road to nowhere as a journey to a place I really didn't wish to go. After all those years, how had it come back to this?

Feminist theorists, pop psychologists, and women's magazines agree on almost nothing, but on this there seems to be a deep and therefore suspect consensus: you have to love yourself, and your life, before you can make a good choice when it comes to another person. Yet at my saddest and most broken—first as a vulnerable young woman, then again in the wake of a rape and kidnapping that had left me feeling more alone than I ever imagined possible—I had chosen Cliff. As much as I wanted to leave my smaller, earlier self behind, it was she—and not the worldlier and "wiser" person I was to become—who had gotten it so right.

I did not know if I wanted to go back to Cliff. I did not even know, more than seven years later, if I could. But somewhere deep inside me, I suspected that I should.

Note to self:

**To get what you really need
you have to be who
you really are.**

In Like

CAMPBELL SMITH

Campbell Smith is a Jack-of-three-trades. (Maybe four, if you count her ability to fold a dinner napkin into a bra.) Born in the bowels of Central Texas—specifically, a cool little hamlet called Austin—she eventually flew the coop and moved to the bustling megalopolis of New York City to become a television producer, sometimes actress, and writer. Following a six-year employment stint at *The Daily Show with Jon Stewart* and far too many stupidly cold winters, Campbell ultimately landed in sunshiny Los Angeles, where she now co-runs Carousel Television, a production company owned by the stunningly talented Steve Carell. She is extremely ungrateful for all of the above and is generally only happy when she gets wind of other people's sadness.

don't know much, good people of the world, but I do know this: if you're a grown woman and you have a very close relationship with a straight man, you two had *better* be doing to ol' humpty dumpty dance if you want to avoid some scathing judgment and a sea of disbelieving eye rolls. It's one of the rare instances in life where you will be judged for *not* having sex. Shame on you for not having sex with that perfectly able straight man! No one has prepared this poor earth, or anyone on it, to handle a purely platonic man-woman relationship—it's unnatural, freakish, weird, and most important, impossible. In short, you are living A LIE.

You may recall in The Best Film Ever Made, Harry told Sally all about this paradox, and she didn't listen. I paraphrase, but he warned her: "The sex part always gets in the way, and therefore the friendship is ultimately doomed." And yes, ultimately, Harry was proven right. They eventually fell madly in love and the "sex part" totally got in the way. *When Harry Met Sally* might be the most memorable telling of a friends-turn-lovers story in recent history, but there are countless others. In nearly every single documented instance where a man and woman begin as "just friends"—whether it is in a movie, a television series, a book, a play, a song, a pamphlet, a memo . . . I think you're catching the drift—it's just not interesting unless they end up in bed doing the horizontal boogie (sometimes, it's even vertical, but that's neither here nor there). But, that's entertainment. Real Life has no idea how to wrap things up with such a pretty little bow.

Case in point: Me. In the late nineties I graduated from what is surely known as "The Harvard of Tallahassee," Florida State University. From there I moved to New York City, and it was there that I met my PLP—that's Platonic Life Partner—Thom. From this point forward, however, to protect his real identity, we will refer to him as "Tom."

Tom can indeed be compared to Harry in this scenario, but the difference is this: Tom and I have not and will not ever make sweet whoopee, spoon by a crackling fireplace, feed each other strawberries, or pick out glassware together. The very idea is gross. No, I think Tom and I would know by now if we were each other's "ones" or, hell, even one hundreds, and it's just not the case. Yet, oddly, our relationship over the years has evolved into something a lot *like* a marriage (though the desire for sex is still about equal to our desire for arsenic pie). We even spend far more quality time together—twenty-four hours a day, give or take an hour—than the average couple, and it sure would be convenient if we *were* in love, but that search continues for us both.

Not only have Tom and I been very close friends for over a decade, we both ultimately moved to Los Angeles, work together (in an office of a mere three employees), and for the past few years, we've even *lived* together. We carpool together, eat together, breathe together, and nearly-everything-else together. In fact, now that I think about it, I think we *have* picked out glassware together . . . I just checked the kitchen; indeed we have. We're also both single, straight, and very much enjoy the idea of finding romantic love. But for whatever reason, not with each other. Obviously, there *is* love there, just a unique kind that can be difficult for people—or even for me—to label. No two people would choose to spend so much of their lives together if there wasn't a foundation of love in some form or another. And how else can you explain the fact that we'll suddenly say things like, "Is Dom DeLuise still alive?" immediately followed by a head-whip and then, "WEIRD!" all at the exact same moment?

A typical Tom and Campbell day involves waking up in our appropriately separate bedrooms, getting ready for work, meeting in one of each other's cars around 9:00 a.m., running a television production company together, and then if it's a rare evening where we don't have to do "work drinks" and schmooze with folks before going home, we play Ping-Pong in our living room. I cannot *tell* you how important Ping-Pong has become to the survival and "thrival" of our friendship. Screw humility. Sometimes we are so selfishly enthralled by how fast and exciting it is that we have to stop to regain our composure from laughing too hard. I am fairly certain either one of us could join the Chinese pro circuit if we had the desire. But my point is that we still find ways to have fun together and laugh. It's the seemingly insignificant things that still matter the most.

While some people question our platonic status, others— including myself—have even broader questions about how our relationship affects our possibilities for love in the future. Will either of us ever find romantic, make-out-in-waves-crashing-upon-the-shore kind of love? Are Tom and I in danger of being each other's "void-fillers" and hindering each other from finding the real thing? The latter is a theory I've heard more than once, and even entertained on occasion. But maybe that's just an excuse; maybe it's normal to have difficulty consciously prioritizing True Love when you live in career-obsessed cities like New York or Los Angeles. In any case, I'm pretty used to the constant bombardment of questions from family and friends along the lines of, "Don't you *want* to fall in love and get married? What's wrong with that wonderful *Tom*?" For the record, yes, I would like to get married; but explaining why I'm not attracted to Tom in that way can be hard for people to understand.

It's not that I find Tom hideous or anything. "The ladies" seem to like him a lot, and I can see why. He's good-looking, confident, funny, and smart. And, sure, he's got his share of flaws like the rest of us, but I often try to analyze the real reason why neither of us finds the other romantically attractive. Of course, looking at it from *his* perspective, I can't come up with one single reason why he isn't attracted to *me*, which makes my analysis even harder.

It could be a simple chemical incompatibility, or our different political and ideological views, or maybe it's due to the circumstances under which we met. Perhaps it's his fourth nipple. (I am not opposed to starting rumors based on blatant lies.) He's also addicted to hookers. Big time.

Speaking of how we met, let's examine how this freakish partnership began. I was twenty-two and had just finished my internship at ABC's groundbreaking, hold-the-phone-amazing television masterpiece *The View*. (Five separate essays could be written about my feelings for Star Jones alone, but I suppose I will have to patiently wait for a book themed on "Hate"). I had also just emerged from an odd string of short-term boyfriends, all of who happened to have porn star names. In chronological order, there had been my college boyfriend, Vince Valentine; the rebound Emmett Rider; and some random guy I met at a bar in New York, Eric Seaman. Let's go over that again, shall we? Vince Valentine, Emmett Rider, and Eric Seaman. I've done the math, and the odds of dating three porn star names in a row are staggering. I consider it one of my proudest accomplishments. But back to how Tom and I met.

I admit, any memory of the *actual* moment is fuzzy at best, but I do know it was by a copy machine. We had both just started working at *The Daily Show with Jon Stewart* in New York City, and were extremely thrilled to have landed our first real television jobs. We had been hired as eager new production assistants, and at some point while I was making copies, we introduced ourselves. I believe he said something mildly amusing like, "Oh nice, a Xerox 4500. If you ever want to know how to open up the bells and whistles on this thing, let me know." Our often sarcastic, often lame, like-minded sense of humor made us fast friends, and this still remains the crusty glue of our long friendship.

Now, I think humans automatically and instinctively assess whether there is any sexual potential from the moment we meet someone new, be it subconscious or otherwise. In my initial meeting of Tom, I recall thinking, *That guy isn't disgusting, per se, and yet I feel that if we became intertwined in a carnal embrace, I would surely barf.* I would like to begrudgingly state that he felt the exact same way about me. The reasoning behind these immediate instincts of mutual sexual repulsion? One possibility: our significant others at the time, Nate and Melissa. Although, to protect their identities, they will hereby be referred to as "Nathan" and "Marissa." Marissa was Tom's longtime, on-and-off again girlfriend, and he wasn't quite done with that chapter yet. And Nathan was my boyfriend at the time, who I met while interning at *The View*. He was the young and sizzly tape coordinator, and holy Lord, did I have a mind-swirling crush on him. I simply had eyes for no one else.

Between my attempts at deflecting insults and insanely divalike demands from Star Jones (avoiding tempting tangent, avoiding tempting tangent), I used to make my days of interning more enjoyable by taking a quick break and inventing reasons to talk to Nathan downstairs. He didn't have a porn star name, so naturally I was skeptical at first, but he had the most

adorable smile, a good sense of humor, and the most adorable smile again. I was smitten in no time. Never in my wild-
est imagination did I think he would be into me, too. In fact,
I was under the impression he didn't like me at all—he was in
no way affectionate or even really *warm* toward me. I was utterly floored when he offered to walk me to the subway station
after work one night, stopped me just before I descended the
platform, and with the snow whipping our faces, told me he had
a crush on me and had been wanting to ask me out for weeks.
God, if I could get my hands on a freeze-frame shot of my face
at that moment. Suddenly, twenty-three degrees and snow felt
quite . . . hot. I tried to sound awesome, but instead stuttered
a "Sure, yeah, cool, okay," and the next eight months were history. Eventually, I listened to the annoyingly wise little voice in
my head, admitted I wasn't in love with Nathan, and broke it
off. But at the time Tom and I first met, I was smack dab in the
middle of the illusion that I might be in love with Nathan. And,
like I said, Tom had his Marissa situation.

Tom and I were both eventually single again, and as we
moved up the work ranks over the months and years together,
we became tighter friends, growing into a non–*Blue Lagoon*
brother–sisterlike duo. He hooked up with my friends, I
hooked . . . hhheld hands with his friends. The situation was
full of perks. On the one hand, it was really nice having him
around to offer a guy's perspective, completely untainted by the
insecurities that romantic involvement brings. On the other
hand, understandably, this closeness posed a few problems for
the poor folks with whom Tom and I got romantically involved.
(Nathan, for one, hadn't been keen on the friendship, and from
his point of view, I'm sure it *was* difficult to be wholly trusting of

the situation.) To this day, it is difficult to convince prospective partners that Tom and I are only friends; but I'm not sure what I would do if I were given an ultimatum to stop seeing Tom. I keep smoke bombs in my purse for this very type of awkward situation. I guess if it ever arose, I'd probably unleash one like a magician and run into the smoky abyss. Thankfully, it usually just takes a bit of time for folks to be around us long enough to realize the dynamic is palpably void of physical attraction, and then our friendship becomes a moot point.

If I'm being really honest (heart-on-my-sleeve alert!), I should point out that *I'm* not usually the one having to convince prospective partners that Tom is only a friend. I had more serious relationships in the fifth grade than I've had in the last five years. I claim to be open to a serious relationship, so what exactly is it that's holding me back from finding something substantial? Does it have anything to do with my closeness to Tom? One commonly held assumption is that men are initially intimidated by my living situation with a straight, single male. Or maybe I'm subconsciously putting out batlike sonar waves declaring myself contentedly unavailable. After all, I have the best of all worlds: Tom fills the surrogate man-in-the-house role and fixes faucets, while I still have the freedom to go out with whomever I want, no strings attached.

In regard to dating, some "helpful" people have suggested that I should try being "less funny," or I should "tone down" my outgoingness and independence. Many guys apparently hate these disgusting qualities. It's not that I don't appreciate the advice, assholes. I do. But finding subtle humor in things and being social and outgoing are as much a part of me as my arms and legs. Even if I tried to contain it, the facade would be shattered soon enough. That advice is the personality equivalent of telling someone to wear a padded bra. Limited roads with both of these shams, believe me.

I suppose I can admit Tom holds some of the most important traits in a man that I look for in a romantic partnership. We not only have similar tastes, compatible humor, and the frightening ability to read each other's minds; he actually seems to appreciate the fact that I am a bit wackier than most women. There is simply an unexplainable understanding and comfort between us, and we genuinely just like being around each other. Heck, we know each other probably more wholly than our families do at this point. Tom could just as easily be described as my Platonic Soul Mate (PSM), but by God, keep your eye on that "P." A big part of that unexplainable bond is the also-unexplainable fact that we recoil at the thought of rolling in the sheets with one another. Maybe our pheromones don't get along, maybe we just work better as friends and it's meant to be this way, or perhaps he was mayonnaise in his former life and I can still sense it. I wish I had an answer for you, but I'll only ever have guesses.

The past few years have not been without a few romances, some of which involved men who actually embraced my alleged personality flaws. My most meaningful and most recent ex, Ryan, whom of course we will refer to as . . . I'm going with "Gerald" this time . . . was so sweetly accepting and encouraging of my humor and largely demureless personality. Which may be partly because he himself was about as tame and contained as a pit bull on acid. In the beginning of our relationship, Gerald was naturally suspicious of my odd friendship with a person donning a penis (although, I prefer to think Tom is like a "Ken" doll down there). But then Gerald met Tom, and to my pleasant surprise, *they* fell platonically in love. In the end, Gerald liked Tom as a dude too much to be suspicious of any wrongdoing. Their bro-mance may have saved the romance (wink, tooth sparkle . . . cough).

Gerald was awesome. He was so affectionate toward me, kind, and loving, but with a hefty dollop of complete and utter insanity. He was an Ivy League educated genius who played college football, which made for a fantastic combination of brains and brawn. But he never quite left the locker room—you know, that scary place where men run around naked, whip each other with towels, and say stupid shit like, "Dude, see how hard you can punch me in the face!" Testosterone is so frightening.

The best example of this occurred when Gerald and I first started getting serious and I decided to take him to my office Christmas party. I was eager to debut the new man. It was a magical night, until approximately 2:30 a.m., when my lady-boss ran up to me and screamed, "Your boyfriend just whipped his *dick* out at me!" then proceeded to run out the door in an offended tizzy. Now, I know what you're thinking. You're thinking, "Gerald whipped his dick out, didn't he?" Yes. Yes, he did. Right after my lady-boss's hasty exit, Tom ran up to me and said calmly, "Don't be mad at him. Don't be mad at him." I glanced over, and took in the most guilty, worried, panicked face I have ever seen on a culprit. Turns out, Gerald had indeed whipped "it" out, and as the story goes, he was (*"so drunk that when she dared me to show her my uncircumcised penis, and babe, she kept daring me—I did! I'm so sorry! I don't know why I do these things!!"*) quite inebriated, and since my boss had dared him to show his uncircumcised penis, he simply did. Apparently, she just refused to believe what was going on "down there," and honestly, you *never* dared Gerald to do anything you didn't want done.

Even though my boss was generally a huge advocate and participant herself in these kinds of party antics, that was by no means an excuse. I was *not* amused by the situation, and Gerald knew it. He cried. He begged me to forgive him. And truth be told, I absolutely believe he was simply missing that certain chip in the brain that tells you when you're being an inappropriate idiot. I actually felt sympathy for this flaw in his wiring. He had a soft and very sincere heart underneath his glitchy exterior.

We came very close to splitting after "The Incident," but I eventually forgave him; we even ended up living together soon thereafter. But after a while, the party antics got tiresome, and I had to make a decision about whether I could live with Gerald's exhausting intensity and unpredictability for the rest of my life. It was the hardest decision I ever made, but the answer was no. Three years after that memorable Christmas party, I broke up with him and his uncircumcised penis. I don't regret one second of that relationship—we really loved each other. Yet I also don't regret breaking up. (However, Tom might regret the breakup a bit. He and Gerald had grown close, and although I never would have asked Tom to stop hanging out with Gerald, they naturally saw each other much less and eventually stopped keeping touch on any regular basis.)

When it comes to support after a breakup, Tom and I are each other's flying buttresses. We're there for each other to lean on, listen to, and vent about how and why things went wrong. Of course, whenever Tom has a breakup, it's easy for me—I simply buy him a hooker. My point is, Tom and I are very open with each other about our relationships. Although that doesn't mean we always just tell each other what we think the other wants to hear. It's honesty galore when it comes to our opinions on suitors and suitees. Both of us always try and befriend the other's main squeeze, but if we start to sense any signs of insufficient awesomeness coming from the other's date, we're not likely to suppress those thoughts. I'm very guilty of biting my lip on a few occasions, however, especially if I saw Tom getting serious with a girl who had that lack of awesomeocity. I loathed one of his longtime girlfriends in particular—*loathed*—but at the end of the day I decided to put on a supportive face for the ultimate sake of my friendship with Tom. I believe Tom would do the same for me, but he'll never have to face that issue because I only date awesome people.

Since the Gerald breakup, I've been single for a while. I've dated here and there, but most days it's just my PLP-n-me . . . and occasionally the hot chick he picks up in a bar and brings home. We're both very encouraging of each other's quests to find True Love, there is zero jealousy, and we genuinely want to support each other's happiness. And yet Tom and I won't live together forever. He is a fantastic roommate and obviously much more than just that, but I think in due time it will be healthy for us both to live on our own again . . . and see each other only fourteen hours a day. To be honest, we're both guilty of feeling oversaturated at times with each other's presence, and who could blame us? All day, every day is a lot of time to spend with Pierce Brosnan, much less your stupid best friend. I would never want our friendship to become stale or an effort to sustain, and I think a healthy balance in all aspects of any relationship is hugely important to its continued endurance. But

Tom and I will continue to love and support each other whether or not we share keys to the same house. What matters is that we have undeniably proven that a man and a woman can really, truly be friends.

Note to self:

**Love comes in many flavors,
and they're all
pretty damn delicious.**

Open Heart

MARIE TILLMAN

Marie Tillman is a writer, advocate, and founder of the Pat Tillman Foundation, a nonprofit organization that invests in veterans and their families through education and community. In the fall of 2008 she began a major national initiative, Tillman Military Scholars, which enables veterans, active service members, and their dependents to fulfill their academic dreams. Her mission is to tell the story of the power, possibility, and devotion of every veteran and military family member. Her memoir about love, loss, and life, entitled *The Letter,* will be released in February 2012 by Grand Central Publishing.

hen I was a young girl, I would flip through my parents' wedding album and dream about getting married. I had a fairy-tale vision of a long white dress, thousands of pink flowers, and a big cake. And in many ways, that dream came true. At twenty-five, I married my childhood love and it was all there: the dress, the flowers, the cake. We stood up in front of our family and friends, swore our love to one another, then drank champagne and danced late into the night, enjoying every minute of our special day. Everything was perfect. But this picturesque life ended shortly after we returned from our honeymoon.

Before we walked down the aisle, my husband Pat had decided to put his career as a football player with the Arizona Cardinals on hold and join the Army. Compelled by the events of 9/11 to take a different path and focus on something that felt more meaningful, he walked away from his life as a professional athlete to serve his country. So, shortly after we returned from Tahiti, still tan from days of kayaking and lying in the sun, he went off to basic training.

In the years that followed, I saw him only sporadically and worried about his safety constantly. We were quickly indoctrinated into the realities of Army life, as he deployed to two war zones in the first eighteen months of his service. Just shy of our two-year wedding anniversary I received the news all military wives fear the most: Pat had been killed, in the desolate mountains of southeastern Afghanistan. In the blink of an eye everything changed, and suddenly I was faced with difficulties I never imagined. The fairy tale was over for good.

After Pat died, I felt his loss everywhere, and in everything. In the 2004 movie *Shall We Dance?* Susan Sarandon's character says, "We need a witness to our lives. There's a billion people on the planet, what does any one life really mean? But in a marriage, you're promising to care about everything. . . . You're saying, 'Your life will not go unnoticed because I will notice it. Your life will not go unwitnessed because I will be your witness.' " After eleven years of being witness to someone's life, and having someone be witness to mine, I was suddenly left alone and felt it deeply.

I mourned Pat's physical presence, the warmth of his body next to me at night in bed; I mourned his friendship, as he was the person whose company I most enjoyed and who I had gone to for over a decade for guidance and advice. I mourned our past, present, and the future we would never have. While my girlfriends read *What to Expect When You're Expecting* to prepare for the new joys in their lives, I read Joan Didion's *The Year of Magical Thinking* to help me cope with my new reality. Without Pat's friendship and partnership, I found the world to be a very lonely place. The fairy tale was gone and I had nothing to replace it. Without him, I drifted, not realizing how much his presence had anchored my life.

I retreated into the deep recesses of my mind. Soon, I realized that if I held on to my childhood visions of how my life was supposed to have turned out, I would never be able to find happiness again. I started to deconstruct all of my former beliefs, questioning everything. I wanted to get to the core of what really mattered to me so I could build a life around those things. I reevaluated everything I thought I believed in, blew apart the notions I'd held closely about what a good life was supposed to look like. Some things rose to the top. Love is certainly one of them—the kind that makes you want to be a better person, the kind that enriches your life and your soul, the kind of love I felt with Pat.

Slowly I started working through the different areas of my life focusing on the things I could handle at the time. I moved away from our home in University Place, Washington, and started a new life in New York City. I found a job in television that I enjoyed and started to meet new friends who filled my life with love and laughter. I dedicated my free time to a nonprofit foundation I started in Pat's name and found great meaning in helping others. A new life started to take shape, and while I still grieved for the past and what should have been, I was working my way toward a happy future. Only one area of my life remained tightly locked away: although friends started encouraging me to date, I still wasn't ready for love.

My relationship with Pat was an enormous part of my identity and happiness, but now the role of wife had been replaced with the role of widow—something I was far less comfortable with. For many years, I couldn't see how anyone else would fit into my life. Having once been so connected to another human being, I longed for that feeling again but didn't think it was possible. I wasn't ready to open my heart to someone else. I kept myself closed off from love, instead finding happiness in family, great friends, and meaningful work.

Eventually, I ventured out into the dating world, but with a much different goal than many of my single friends. I wasn't looking for love or marriage. After several years alone with my grief, I was looking for fun—easy, light relationships I could move in and out of without pain or complication. After a few awkward first dates and a bit of a rocky start, these relationships became surprisingly easy, but the fun was short-lived. I soon realized that without depth or attachment, these encounters felt hollow. I wasn't cut out for casual affairs, and while I longed for a deeper connection, my heart was still guarded. I knew if I found someone, my feelings would be different than they were with Pat, but I could still find something deep and meaningful; relationships, like fingerprints, are uniquely special. Maybe I could even find love. But I was no longer sure about marriage.

I had loved being married, happily changed my name, and took on the role of wife with delight. I loved the commitment that it symbolized, the security I felt making things official. And after over eight years together, it had felt right. Still, I was quite young when I got married, and now that I was a little older, and friends around me started going through painful divorces, I began to look at the institution of marriage differently. I realized that as a twenty-five-year-old bride, my childhood views on marriage had been all I knew, but I now see many healthy variations on this theme. I have several friends who have been with their partners for decades but never married. Some have children, some don't, but in most cases they are just as committed to each other as people who have entered into the traditional union I know from my childhood, minus the slip of paper.

Having been married and widowed before the age of thirty made me question things in life a little more. I no longer blindly followed tradition or in the footsteps of my parents. After years of self-exploration and discovery, I cobbled together a life that had meaning for me. I have always felt that a shared life is a happy life, and I value the closeness between two committed people. I hope to find that connection again someday, but I'm just not sure I will need a piece of paper to validate this most intimate of relationships.

I no longer have visions of a long white gown and a fairy-tale ending, but love I still believe in, as well as the wonder of two people joined together in the journey of life. Maybe love is felt more deeply with the traditional commitment of marriage, maybe not. Who could possibly say for sure?

I don't know if I'll get married again someday, but I do know it will be under no false illusions, or fairy-tale visions. There is no way to tell where life will end up, but for now, after many dark years with my heart locked away, I'm proud to walk back out into the world openhearted and ready for love.

Note to self:

**Love is not a piece of paper,
it's a piece of your heart.**

"Then He Smiled at Me, Pa Rum Pum Pum Pum"

KATHLEEN WILHOITE

Kathleen Wilhoite was born and raised in Santa Barbara, California. After high school she moved to L.A. to attend USC's program for drama and landed an acting job three weeks later. She's been acting ever since. Most notably, she played Chloe on *ER* and gave her baby away while singing on *Cop Rock*. She got her first record deal when she was twenty-four years old with Polygram, and opened for acts such as Ziggy Marley and Kenny Loggins. She is currently fine-tuning her novel, *Locked Out,* and recently completed her one-woman show, *Stop Yelling in My Ear.* She lives in Los Angeles with her three kids and husband.

I couldn't help but notice Dave's biceps when he lifted his kick drum out of the backseat of his maroon 1982 Cadillac Coupe de Ville, and by the time he bent over to lift the snare off the floor of the front seat I'd fallen in love.

I've always had a thing for drummers. My first husband was a drummer. Too bad they don't have a "lemon law" for husbands, because my ex was a lemon, and I should have gotten a refund. Eighteen months after we'd married, the divorce was final; he embarked on a path to sobriety, and I was lucky enough to get my recording career back on track, vowing, of course, never to have anything to do with another drummer.

So there I was, once again, helping a drummer load in his drums for a session. *So much for vows*, I thought.

We recorded a song I'd written for my friend's movie well into the night, and at one point, while playing with amazing sensitivity, Dave looked at me in the vocal booth and started making heavy-metal-rock faces, twirling his sticks, and head-banging. I cracked up. Then close to the end of the session, in a moment of frustration, he pretended to hit himself in the head with a drumstick while simultaneously playing the kick drum. I liked this guy. He was cute, smart, funny, and talented. I was twenty-nine years old, with my clock ticking, and my broken heart mended. I was ready to get out there and start dating.

After the session, I followed him out to his car. He was carrying a couple of toms, and I had his bag of sticks. "Hey, you got a girlfriend?" I asked.

He was struggling to get the toms in the backseat over his kick drum. "No," he said, then turned around and smiled. "Why?"

"I like the way you play," I said.

He nodded. "Okay."

I nodded. "Drums. I like the way you play drums."

"Thanks."

"Want to go on a date?" With that, the casual nature of our conversation came to a screeching halt.

He cocked his head and said, "Did you just ask me out on a date?"

"Yes."

"I don't date," he said.

"What do you mean?"

"I don't date."

"How do you get to know anyone?"

"I don't know. I play a club, have a few drinks, pick up a chick, and take her home. I don't know what I do, but I know I definitely don't . . . date."

"So that's it?" I asked. "Am I ever going to see you again?"

"Yeah, probably." He got in his car, and as he drove off he yelled out the window, "Hey, I liked your song."

I walked back to my car thinking, *Kath, if you don't want to be single, you'll need to ask people out. You did the right thing.* I didn't want to wait around like a flower waits for the bees; there was always a chance that by the time the bees got around to it, the poor flower's insides would have withered up, her thighs would have puckered, and her boobs would have sagged. But Dave's "I don't date" proclamation had me questioning my approach. I owned my own home and had a record deal; I wasn't used to getting rejected in such a straightforward way. My bold attempt at landing a date with him having failed, I decided to ease into things by asking him to join my band. I had a show coming up and needed a new drummer anyway.

I called Dave the next day. He said yes to joining my band. *Maybe he was just tired when I asked him out, or was in a bad mood after the recording session,* I thought. I then figured it was the word "date" that he objected to, so I was more specific this time and asked if he wanted to see the midnight show of *Reservoir Dogs* at the Beverly with me. He said no.

The following week, after rehearsal, I thought, *What if he's already seen that movie or isn't into Quentin Tarantino?* So I asked him out again. Again, he said no. The day after that, I decided to do things his way. He was filling in with Eudipus and the Mothers at the Troubador that night, so I suggested I meet him there. He could have a few drinks, pick up a chick and take her home, only the chick—would be me. He laughed and said no. The following day, I went back to my clunky standby: "Are you sure you don't want to go on a date with me?" He said yes. At our remaining rehearsals, I asked him out over and over again, phrasing it differently each time, and each time he said no. I knew I was making a nuisance of myself, but I couldn't stop. He kept smiling at my stupid jokes and the nature of our conversations during our smoke breaks seemed to contradict his insistence on not wanting to date me. I was stumped.

On the day of the show, as we were loading in, he passed by me in the wings. I decided to ask him out one last time. He pretended not to hear me, so I asked him out during sound check, speaking right into the microphone, my voice booming into the large venue.

"Testing one, two. One, two. Check, check," I said. "Check, check, testing—Dave. Will you please go on a date with me?" I turned around for his answer.

He did a rim shot and shook his head. The guys in the band laughed. Now, my asking him out had become a running gag. I promised myself I wouldn't do it anymore, but after the show, he was sitting on the couch in the green room, looking so cute in his Ramones T-shirt, balancing a beer on his head and playing drums on his abs. I asked him out in earnest, one final, that's-it-I'm-never-asking-again, last-chance time.

He said yes. Only he phrased it more like, "Okay. I'll go out with you, if you'll just stop asking me."

Date night arrived. I lit candles and dressed up like Joan Jett in anticipation of his arrival. The doorbell rang, echoing through the empty rooms of the new house I'd just bought with my record deal money. (Unfortunately, I'd run out of cash after the down payment and couldn't afford much furniture.)

I opened the door. "Come on in," I said, gesturing like Carol Merrill from *Let's Make a Deal.* "Welcome to my humble abode."

He laughed and made some crack about how there was nothing humble about it, then he sang the theme from *Miami Vice* and asked me where I hid my plastic flamingos. Interior/exterior design had never been my forte, and I'd gotten a little carried away with the whole turquoise/gray/pink/black palette that was popular in the late eighties, my heyday.

We cooked dinner together, hung out, and the next thing I knew, it was two o'clock in the morning and we were downstairs in my music room playing bad renditions of Beatles songs.

I was having fun, but more than that I was impatient and horny. "Hey, Dave," I said. "Pull up a milk crate." We sat knee to knee. "Listen, it seems clear to me that we get along, right?"

"Right," he said.

"I think you're cute, smart, funny, and talented. You meet all of my criteria."

"And I think you're one of the coolest chicks I've hung out with in a long time."

"Okay." I nodded my head. "So?"

He shrugged. "Yeah?"

I blurted, "Do you want to make out?"

"Uh . . ."

My confidence seeped out of me like the air from a punctured tire. I muttered, "Yeah. Weird, huh? Weird that I asked like that. Lame, really. I don't know why I did that. I totally understand if you don't want to, believe me. I'm a flawed person. There are a ton of things wrong with me. I'm shaped like a human bowling pin for one thing, so I get it, but I'm kinda nice and I have a pretty good, not great, but solid singing voice, so there's that." I was on the edge of my milk crate at this point. "So do you?"

"Do I what?"

"Do you do want to make out?"

He squinted. It looked like he was considering it. He nodded. I was thrilled, until the nod slowly turned into . . . oh, good Lord, he was going to say no again. *Our evening has to end right here, before he says it*, I thought. *Stop! Poof, go away! Be gone. You're a toad. I'm a princess. I hope the earth opens up, you fall in, and it closes back up again.*

"Nah," he said.

"Nah?" I asked. "Really?"

"Naah." He gave me a longer "Nah" that time. But it was a clear-as-a-bell "Nah," no doubt about it.

" 'Nah,' " I said, "like, when someone asks, 'Hey, do you want to play Chinese jump rope?' and the other person says, 'Nah'—that kind of 'nah'?"

He didn't have an answer.

I felt like I'd been kicked in the solar plexus. Blabbermouth that I can be at times, I was at a total loss for words. Then I heard myself bust out with a fake laugh. "That's so funny," I said. "I must be going deaf because I could have sworn you'd just said, 'Nah,' after I'd asked you to make out."

He laughed at the old "I must be going deaf" bit, which I tend to do whenever anyone says something I don't like.

"Well, it's late," he said. "I should be going."

Neither of us said a word on the long walk back to my front door. I opened the door for him, and for a few seconds we stood awkwardly at the threshold.

"Well, 'bye," he said and gave me a friendly punch in the arm. "See ya around, dude."

I watched his taillights shrink in the darkness as he drove away. Then I closed the door, and dragged my sad ass up four flights of stairs to the top floor, where I gazed out my fourteen-foot plate-glass window at the lights on the Capitol Records building and the Roosevelt Hotel sign. I felt like the ugliest girl on earth. I opened the sliding glass door, stepped out onto the balcony, and thought, *I could always jump. End it all. Finally stop humiliating myself.* I looked down onto the sloped mountain-side. I was four stories up. It wasn't high enough. I wouldn't die if I jumped. I'd be maimed for life and become a burden to my family. My poor mother would end up being my caretaker. I imagined myself in a wheelchair, sipping a protein shake out of a straw stuck in the side of my mouth, and my mother standing over me, saying, "You're so selfish, Kathy. All you do is think about yourself, and ya wear that black all the time. You're really letting yourself go. No wonder you don't have a man. You should do musicals. You were never as good as you were when you played Reno Sweeny in *Anything Goes* at Santa Barbara High School . . ."

Oh, no. Fuck that. I wasn't jumping.

Dave and I had one last obligation that would force us to be in each other's company: we had agreed to go to the wedding of a mutual friend. My plan was to give him until midnight to make a move. I thought, if that clock strikes twelve and nothing's happened, he's officially out. I didn't want any more male friends. I had too many as it was, and it made me feel like a fishwife. I didn't need to be another hot guy's "buddy." No kiss by midnight, and he was out of my band and out of my life. I arrived at the wedding, sour-faced and ready to just barrel through.

Dave greeted me at the church. He sat next to me in the pew. We whispered funny comments to each other throughout the ceremony. Afterward, at the reception, he pulled out my chair, and later, got me a piece of wedding cake. The Circle Jerks played. He drank; I smoked; we pogo'd; we moshed. We had a great time. It was still early as the party wound down, and he asked me to meet him at El Conquistador for dinner. When we were seated at the restaurant, he dipped a tortilla chip in the salsa and fed it to me. There were a few awkward moments, but not many. Afterward, we went back to his apartment and watched *The Simpsons* with his two roommates.

At some point, I looked up at the Sid Vicious clock over the mantel and saw that he had about a minute to spare. "It's almost midnight," I said, getting up with a heavy sigh. "I've got to split." I walked over to his Barcalounger and put my hand on his shoulder. I was hoping he'd grab it and pull me around so I could sit on his lap, and we'd make out right there in front of God and his two roommates, but it didn't happen. The big hand on the clock clicked on the twelve right between Sid Vicious's eyes. Midnight. Game over. He was a pumpkin and I was an ashy Cinderella.

I walked over to the front door. "See ya," I said.

At that moment, Chief Wigham, a character on *The Simp-*

sons, rolled down a hillside in a beer costume, and Dave cracked up. I guess he hadn't heard me, or didn't care that I was leaving because he never got up.

"Oh, no. Don't bother," I said sarcastically. "I'll let myself out." I closed the door behind me and walked down the hill to my car, bouncing on my toes, trying to cheer myself up. I couldn't feel my legs, just tears, cool on my cheeks in the night air.

I unlocked my car and was about to get in when I heard "Kathleeeeeen!" in the distance. I looked up and saw Dave running down the street.

"What?" I said, quickly wiping my face on my sleeve.

He walked up, put his hands on my neck, and kissed me. I started to pull away, thinking this had to be some sort of sick joke, but he leaned me back against the car and kissed me again.

My knees were weak, my breathing shallow, my pulse racing. I thought, *Oh, good Lord, I'm going to have an orgasm.*

"What?" he said.

I shook my head, horrified I might have made a cheesy porn chick noise.

"What did you say?" he asked again.

I wanted to answer him with words that were deep and profound, meaningful, something neither of us would ever forget. But all that came out was, "What took you so long, Fucker?"

"I like you too much," he said. "I like you too much to just have sex with you, Kath. We could have fucked that night, but I like you too much. I wanted to be sure."

"Aw, Shakespeare, you flatter me," I said and resisted the huge urge to act like my trampy self. I got in my car. "See ya around, sailor," I said and drove home. Every time I hit a pothole or drove over a speed bump, it would jog my short-term memory of his body leaning into mine, his soft lips, his strong hands—and I'd swoon.

We hung out every day after that night. At the time, I had no idea why, but I'd feel actual heat emanating from his body when his knee touched mine under the table at a restaurant, or when he'd pass by me in the hallway at the rehearsal hall. But three months later, after I peed on the little pregnancy stick revealing a positive result, it all made sense. I wouldn't say I believe in soul mates, but I believe that each relationship has its own life span, a beginning, a middle, an end, like a song. My ex-husband and I never made it past the first few bars—we were out of time and off key. But Dave and I found "the pocket," a term musicians use to describe when a song has a sweet feel and a good groove, and no one can pinpoint exactly why. The pregnancy was our first verse into the birth of our son, Jimmy, who became the first chorus, that then flowed into the birth of our daughter Ruby, the second verse, and chorus two was when the four of us traveled to Ethiopia to pick up our third child, Adugna, to round out our family for the bridge, the chorus, and the vamp out into the next song.

Note to self:

Love has many notes;
the fine-tuning is up to you.

Charlie Wilson's Wife

BARBARA WILSON

Barbara Wilson is a trained classical ballet dancer. She's the first graduate of the Washington School of Ballet and was a principal dancer for a number of years. She was a soloist with the Pennsylvania Ballet Company and then with the Harkness Ballet in New York. She taught ballet in the Washington area for twenty-seven years. She's the proud mother of two daughters and currently lives in Washington, D.C.

My life with Charlie Wilson was a series of breathtaking moments, heartbreaking choices, and eleven years and eight days of pure bliss that almost didn't happen. If I didn't believe in God, I would have to conjure up some other magical entity who is in charge of destiny and controls the puppet strings that cause two people to cross paths, separate for years, and then find one another again. Because I know in my heart it was divine intervention that brought us together *both* times and allowed my cautious heart to love bigger than I thought possible.

I grew up in Washington, D.C., where I studied classical ballet and would later dance with the Washington Ballet, and then move on to the Pennsylvania Ballet, before ending up in New York, dancing with the Harkness Ballet. I met my first husband when I was fifteen years old and living in D.C. He was a life-guard at a community swimming pool and we had a young love kind of courtship before I left the D.C. area to travel with the ballet. When I returned, five years later, we got married, got to work on a family, and had two beautiful daughters, Sarah and Rachel.

I was incredibly happy in that relationship and had every intention of being married to him for the rest of my life. But when he was thirty-three, he was diagnosed with leukemia and died very suddenly thereafter. Sarah was eight and Rachel was four. I was only twenty-nine, and suddenly a devastated widow and a single mom alone in the world. My husband and I didn't have a life insurance policy, or any savings to speak of; we were young and had been living paycheck to paycheck. When he died, the money rattling around at the bottom of my purse was pretty much all that I had. It was an excruciatingly hard time, and there was hardly any chance to grieve my incredible loss. I had to feed my children and I had to do it fast.

I taught ballet as a means of income, and even though it wasn't a huge paycheck, it's what I loved, and it was enough to put food on the table. I was able to sell my husband's car and put some money in the bank. My daughters would come to work with me every day after they got out of school, watch television, do homework, and have dinner in the dressing room of the ballet studio. Even though Sarah was still very young, she was a great babysitter to Rachel, and without her help I don't know how I would have managed. This was our routine for many years; it was exhausting and it certainly wasn't ideal, but I had no choice. I was focused on one thing at that time in my life: getting through the day with my children fed and a roof over their heads. Dating was out of the question. I had lost the only man I ever thought I would love.

One day, the ballet studio where I worked got a phone call from the National Women's Democratic Club, which was organizing a very large fund-raiser to take place at Arena Stage in Washington, D.C. They needed a choreographer to teach the wives of some of the congressmen four elaborate numbers to different show tunes. I took the assignment, and twice a week, I would go downtown and work with the women. When they found out I was a widow, it became their mission to find me someone to love. As they were going through their black books and chatting about all the men who were eligible, they shared a collective mission statement: "Whatever we do, we've got to keep her away from Charlie Wilson." I had no idea who Charlie Wilson was, much less any clue about his reputation, but I wanted nothing to do with him based on their insistence that he was barricade-worthy. Instead, they set me up with a congressman who shall remain nameless. The date didn't work out at all, to say the least. I thought to myself, *I may not know who Charlie Wilson is, but there's absolutely no way he could be worse than this drunken congressman.* The next time the wives tried to set me up, I politely made myself unavailable. No way was I going down that road again.

After about four months of dance rehearsal, the big event was finally upon us. We had a dress rehearsal the day before, and as I was working with the wives, taking them through their choreography one last time, I saw out of the corner of my eye a tall and handsome man walk into the room. He was the Marlboro Man's doppelganger and I was speechless at the sight of him. When we broke for lunch, he came over and introduced himself as Charlie Wilson. I just about fell over. As it turned out, Charlie was the designated emcee for the evening and so we spent the rest of the day together, going through dress rehearsal. He certainly didn't come across as threatening; in fact, he was kind, hilarious, and incredibly handsome.

Three weeks after we met, he called me up and asked me out. I was so nervous about going on a date with the now-infamous Charlie Wilson that I made up an excuse about why I had to decline. I couldn't believe I didn't accept. He called again, and I said no a second time. By the third time he called, I had run out of excuses, so I told the truth, which was that my girlfriend was staying with me for the weekend. He said, "Great, I'll take you both out." And so my girlfriend, Joyce, chaperoned our first three dates.

As it turned out, the congressional wives had Charlie Wilson all wrong. He was a kind man, full of grace and endless amounts of charm. After the third date, as we were getting into the car, Joyce had the good sense to pull me aside and say, "Barbara, what's wrong with you? He's handsome. He's a gentleman. You're going to be fine. Go out with him on your own." And so I did. He didn't try to kiss me for four months. He said he knew I would be worth the wait. To say I was madly in love is an understatement.

I wasn't the only one in love with Charlie. To know him was to love him. He had movie star charm, a larger-than-life personality, and an altruistic heart. These incredible qualities served him well in his lifelong career in politics. In 1961, he was elected to the Texas State House of Representatives, and for twelve years he fought for a minimum wage increase, Medicare for the poor, and was one of the few prominent Texas politicians who was pro-choice. In 1973, he set his sights on D.C. and was elected to the U.S. House of Representatives, where he served twelve terms.

When I first met Charlie in 1978, he had been in the political machine long enough to gain a ladies' man reputation and for his first marriage to fail. But when he was with me, he was honest and faithful, and I never mistrusted him. We dated for three years, taking things slow. I had young kids who needed stability, and it was my job to provide them with that. He was coming out of a messy divorce and entering into a world that would change his life forever.

Still, being with Charlie made me realize that I wanted to be married again. But I didn't just want to be *a* wife; I wanted to be *Charlie's* wife, even though I knew deep down in my soul he wasn't ready yet. The hardest thing I've ever done was to arrange to meet him at the House Dining Room in D.C. for lunch. When I was with him I was always worried about my girls, and when I was with my girls I was miserable without him, and I just knew we couldn't go on the way we were. I knew that leaving him was ultimately the right thing to do for my children and for me, and still, I must have been in a state of shock, because I don't remember what I said. But Charlie certainly did. According to him, I pushed back my chair in a very bold way and said, "Play me or trade me." I do, however, remember his response. It was like a knife in my heart to hear what I knew was the truth. He feared that if he married me, it would end badly, and he didn't want to hurt me. I left the dining room in tears and I cried for three days straight. I didn't stop to eat. I didn't stop to sleep. I barely stopped to breathe. On day four, I wiped my eyes, blew my nose, and went on with my life. But my heart was never going to be the same.

It was 1980 when I ended my relationship with Charlie. The end of us took place at the beginning of his long fight for the people of Afghanistan against the Soviets. In the process of getting on with my life, I met my second husband, and got married. Looking back on it, I realize I was never quite in love with him, but I desperately wanted to provide a two-parent home for my girls. I was working fifty hours a week teaching ballet, raising my children, and making deals with a husband with a Jekyll and Hyde personality. Meanwhile, unbeknownst to me, Charlie's life was filled with top-secret CIA meetings, trips to Pakistan, and making deals that would ensure hundreds of millions of dollars went to Afghan soldiers fighting the Soviets.

Later, I would learn that Charlie continued to earn a reputation that would precede him everywhere he went, and during that time, a journalist by the name of George Crile started writing a book about him. Charlie thought the book would never see the light of day, and gave George an all-access pass into his world. There were boozy nights in hot tubs, allegations of cocaine use, lots of women, and most important, there was what would become Charlie's legacy: the Afghanistan–Soviet war that he single-handedly helped end. The book was titled *Charlie Wilson's War.*

I didn't keep tabs on him—it was too painful—so I had no idea what was going on in his life or the worlds he was changing. I often saw his secretary, however, and when she asked me how I was doing, I always told her everything was great. I was lying.

About five years after Charlie and I separated, I returned home from running errands one day to find a package on my front step. The minute I saw it, I knew it was from him. When I opened the box, there was a beautiful black beret with a note that said: "This was sent from an admirer." I loved it, and I wore it everywhere. It was my little secret that kept me connected to him and what we once had. That was the only time I ever heard from him, the only time I knew without a doubt he had been thinking of me, although I had a gut feeling I was on his mind just as much as he was on mine.

Another five years passed, and my younger daughter, Rachel, entered the Army and was called to fight in Operation Desert Storm in the Kuwait desert. At the news of her upcoming deployment, I became catatonic. There are no words to describe the pain a parent feels when they see their child go off to war. My heart goes out to every parent who deals with this and the anxiety they live with every day until their child comes home.

I knew that Rachel had entered into a world that was dangerous, and she could possibly lose her life. I begged her not to go. She promised to stay in touch, but if for some reason she couldn't call me every week or so to check in, I was not to worry.

By hook or by crook, I somehow raised a woman who has bravery beyond my scope of understanding. I don't know where she got it, but she truly embodies courage. I had to trust that she would be able to survive, but though we as a family had survived so much already, this was by far the hardest thing I had faced. For the first few months she was away, I heard from Rachel every week like she promised. And then a couple of weeks went by and she went radio silent. About this time, there was a news report that a girl in the Army had been captured, and I became hysterical. It was definitely my Shirley MacLaine moment, where "Find my baby, find my baby" was all I could say, and sometimes scream.

My husband insisted that I call Charlie to see if he could find out anything about Rachel's whereabouts. I didn't want to—I didn't think it was fair after not communicating all that time to ask a favor of him, but ultimately finding my baby trumped any uncomfortable feelings. Three days later, after I spoke to Charlie, the phone rang. It was Rachel. A jeep had pulled up to her camp, which was in an area too remote for outside contact, and driven her three hours to where she could call me, before driving her the three hours back to camp. Charlie had made that happen. I called his office to thank him and my gratitude was expressed at lightning speed with no fanfare. I said, "Charlie, thank you very much for finding Rachel. I'll never forget what you did." And then I hung up. Later he would jokingly say, "At least you could have bought me lunch."

Another five years passed, and my marriage didn't get better. I knew that I was in a bad one, I just couldn't find a way out. As I was contemplating this, my friend Carol ran into Charlie at a bar in D.C. and they had a drink. They started talking about people they loved in their lives, and he said, "There's only one woman I've ever really loved and that was Barbara." Carol couldn't wait to tell me this, and I just about collapsed when I heard it. A few months later, I found out that my husband was having an affair. There was my way out. I walked out the door and never looked back.

When I told Carol that my marriage was over, she immediately called Charlie to let him know. It didn't take him long to pick up the phone. He called and insisted that I come and have dinner with him. As much as I loved him, I almost said no because I was afraid to get hurt again. However, I knew that excuse wasn't going to hold up. And like our previous first date, I insisted on a chaperone (this time it would be Carol). I was secretly hoping that I would see him and wonder, *What was I thinking?* But that didn't happen. He was just as wonderful seventeen years later. And as if no time had passed, we fell back into each other's arms and began again. This time I was older, my children were out of the house, and I could handle it.

Soon after that dinner, we became inseparable. After about five months of dating, on October 31, 1999, as we were sitting in front of the fire at Charlie's house reading, he looked up at me and said, "You know what I think we oughta do? I think we oughta get married." I thought it was a trick-or-treat or some sort of joke. To this day, I don't understand why he picked me. What we had was so peaceful, and this time around, I certainly wasn't in any rush to get married again. I had planned to find myself an apartment, teach ballet, and go to the movies; marriage was not on my agenda. But this was Charlie, and my dream of becoming his wife, a dream that had begun so many years ago, was finally coming true.

During our almost twenty-year hiatus, Charlie had lived the life of twenty men. He was the person credited with turning the tide in the Afghanistan-Soviet conflict and making the Russians leave the country. It was simply due to his intelligence and ability to work through the system and get things done. The book that George Crile had begun about Charlie in the eighties was still in the works and it chronicled both his hand in Afghanistan and his personal life. Charlie warned me of the contents, but he still doubted it would ever be published. He wasn't wrong about much, but he was wrong about that book. *Charlie Wilson's War* not only hit the shelves, it was a huge attention-getter and immediate bestseller. Tom Hanks's company snatched up the film rights, and the subsequent movie came out in 2007 with Hanks playing Charlie and Julia Roberts playing Joanne Herring.

It was one thing to hear about all the escapades from Charlie, and another thing to read it in print; but it was something else altogether to see it on the screen. It was really difficult for me, not for any other reason than how it portrayed the man I loved. He wasn't without fault, of course, but the guy in that book, and in the movie, was not the man I knew. There was also a perception by the public, based on how the movie portrayed them, that Joanne Herring was Charlie's true love, which just wasn't the case. She was vital with regards to Afghanistan and she's an amazing woman in that way, but she was never engaged to him, and he certainly didn't long for her all those years. Their affair, which lasted only a couple of months in real life, was played up because the filmmakers had a superstar in Julia Roberts, and it made for better drama. Now, because of the film, the general public believes Charlie constantly womanized, never settled down, and forever pined for Joanne. It was an artistic license the filmmakers took, and something I've had to live with. The night of the premiere, Tom Hanks came over and gave me a big hug; I think he knew that it was an uncomfortable time for me, and I appreciated his concern.

Amidst all the excitement that a Hollywood premiere brings, there was also an overwhelming feeling of gratitude and relief that Charlie was able to walk down the red carpet, as just two months earlier he had undergone a heart transplant in Houston, Texas. His years of cardiomyopathy had taken their toll, and in July 2007 Charlie was told that he needed a new heart or he would die. The doctors said to expect six to eight months on a waiting list, but within a short forty days, we got the call. We were not prepared for it emotionally, it was all so fast. And just like in the movies, they airlifted him in the middle of the night from our hometown of Lufkin to Houston to transplant the thirty-five-year-old donor's heart into Charlie's seventy-four-year-old body. It was amazing and terrifying all at once, and just two and a half months later, after a grueling recovery process, Charlie was posing for photographers at a glamorous Hollywood premiere of a movie based on his own life. It was pretty spectacular, and we truly believed he had a new lease on life.

Unfortunately, the high from Hollywood didn't last long. During those months and years after his heart transplant, his quality of life suffered dramatically. He always felt sick and tired, or, as he said, "not right." In truth, he felt more like a person with heart disease when he had the new heart than he did when he had his own. I knew something wasn't right, as did he, but we made the best of it. But two and a half years after the transplant, on February 10, 2010, Charlie died suddenly of a heart attack. He was seventy-six years old. We had been married eleven years and eight days.

Charlie was laid to rest at Arlington National Cemetery in a graveside service with full military honors on February 23. In a statement, Robert Gates, U.S. defense secretary, said: "America has lost an extraordinary patriot whose life showed that one brave and determined person can alter the course of history."

But I had lost my hero and my love. There's not a moment

CHARLIE WILSON'S WIFE 263

that goes by that I don't miss him. He was the love of my life. Charlie used to joke about how when he married me, he got his Medicare card and his marriage license in the same year. And a day never went by that I didn't tell him how happy I was that he picked me and made me Mrs. Charlie Wilson, because being Charlie Wilson's wife was more perfect than any Hollywood ending.

Note to self:

**If love is real, it waits,
no matter what.**

$\mathcal{T}he \; \mathcal{P}ang$

LEE WOODRUFF

Lee Woodruff is a freelance writer and coauthor of the *New York Times* bestseller *In an Instant* and the book *Perfectly Imperfect—A Life in Progress*. Woodruff is also a family and lifestyle contributor for *Good Morning America*. She is married to ABC News correspondent Bob Woodruff, and together they have founded ReMind.org, to help wounded service members and their families heal and move forward after the wounds of war. They live in Westchester County, New York, with their four children.

still get that little pang when I see you." My husband says this to me every now and then when he walks in the door and sees me. And even if I'm mad at him—even if I'm standing there with my hands on my hips, head cocked to one side—it still makes me smile. Hearing it stops me right in my tracks because there really isn't anything else he could say that would make me feel so completely . . . loved.

The "pang" is the equivalent of a sizzle. You know that feeling. At least I hope you do. It's the sensation of things flipping

over a little bit inside you, somewhere down below your belly
button. It's what happens when you think about him or her,
when you contemplate and anticipate the night to come or re-
play the one you just had. At my age, maybe the pangs aren't
quite so dramatic. They're more like pulse points. They simply
let you know that the heart is still alive and kicking.

The fact that my husband and I have been married for
twenty-three years and he is still "panging" should be reason
enough to keep him around. Whatever he's done, like leaving
his dry cleaning stubs on my dresser (two feet from the waste-
basket) or making me repeat something for the third time because he is only partially listening (my voice is white noise),
these things seem vastly less important when he pangs.

Marriage is a tough gig. Take two people who are desperately
in love and full of lust and then shackle them together through
the years. The "I can't wait to get him in bed" feeling begins to
evolve into "If that bastard snores again I'm going to stuff the
pillow down his throat." The candlelit meals and champagne
toasts with entwined arms ultimately give way to the routine of
unloading the dishwasher. It's inevitable. Marriage is about the
business of living; of living together and making it work. There
is nothing romantic about a clump of hair in a shared bathroom
shower drain or feeding a family of six night after night. But
this routine becomes a kind of necessary glue that helps it all
hang together. For most of us, anyway.

My husband is easy on the eyes. People are always telling
me how handsome he is. And as smitten as I was by all facets
of him when we first started dating, I chose to give my heart
to someone who would always challenge me intellectually, who
got my sense of humor, and who could, in turn, make me laugh.

I married a kind man, which was vital to me. But most important, I married someone with whom I imagined I would never, ever, have to sit across from forty-five years later at a Denny's buffet, chewing slowly and with absolutely nothing left to say. And after all, handsome is as handsome does. You stop seeing the outside after a while, so you'd better love what's inside.

So, how do folks keep a marriage going? What are the secrets, the keys, the things people do? I get asked this a lot, especially from younger people who seem to think that Bob and I have it all figured out. But I'm loath to be a poster child for matrimony. I know this: there is no perfect marriage. You need mutual respect, the ability to compromise and negotiate, love in all kinds of doses, a few shared dreams, a long leash, and a big sense of humor. Laughter is key. Laugh together, laugh often, laugh when you want to cry, and laugh at yourself. When you are in it for the long haul, self-deprecation and a dose of humility become as sexy as George Clooney. And when the chips are down or you hit a rough patch, gallows humor can ease you through many of the tough times. It's much harder for the heart to break when you're laughing out loud.

I think in the end, as my husband says, you can simply get lucky. You can't possibly predict how someone is going to grow or evolve (or not) in the years to come. You don't necessarily think about the genetic time bombs of cancer, Alzheimer's, or depression that can lurk in the ancestral closet of your combined gene pools or the way your lover was parented (or not) as a child. These are things that will occur to you later. Sometimes, they'll be enough to stop you in your tracks.

It's fairly easy to trace the ways that love can erode. Being a responsible adult is sobering. There are taxes and credit card bills and mortgages, and then you add kids and dishes and laundry, and you find yourself talking out loud about "pee" and "poopy" and germs and telling everyone to "wash your hands" or "it's only funny until someone loses an eye." You begin repeating the inane phrases your mother did—the ones you swore you'd never say—until you realize you've somehow managed to *become* your mother.

With motherhood comes the amazing physical ability to love, nurture, and parent, and you discover that your body is a harbor, a food source, a shelter . . . but a Wonderland? Not so much. You are all touched out. You have held and coddled and consoled and nursed and hugged and physically cajoled, and by the time your man comes home at night searching for a little nookie, offering your body to one more human feels akin to organ donation.

With a job, four kids, and two dogs, there are nights now at age fifty that I'd rather lower myself into an aquarium of hungry piranhas than offer myself up to this man I love. Getting eaten alive by fish is at least passive. It requires very little exertion on my part. (And this is coming from a woman who loves her husband.) Okay, maybe that last part was a little harsh, but getting down on all fours and purring like a kitten is about the last thing on my list after a long day of taking care of everyone and everything else.

In the beginning you might believe that love has the power to help you change someone; make them better, deeper, more sensitive, more compatible. You believe there is a perfect yin to your yang. And love *does* have power to change some things, at least to a degree. But you can't really change them deep down. Not fundamentally, anyway. That part has already been molded, the foundation laid years before you came on the scene. You might train them to hang up their clothes and make their beds, to grill and take out the garbage. But the really important stuff, like your philosophy on raising kids, your religion, or your desire to backpack in Third World countries, those things can be harder to compromise on. So you'd better look closely, and hopefully you'll get lucky too. After all, there's a big dose of luck in this "forever after" stuff.

Time, life, routine, and details become the sandpaper, the emory board that can wear love down in a marriage, leaving a couple shaking their heads and wondering how it slipped away. And so every once in a while you need to pick your marriage up by the seams and shake it, examine it, talk about it, worry about it. You need to face it down. As hard as it may be to find the time, it's important to set it aside, draw a circle on your calendar, put in the hard work to buff up the mutual respect, the sense of humor, and the ability to admit when you're wrong and say, "I'm sorry," when you are. You need to systematically interrupt the business of living and go to work to shore up the edges—before it gets to the point where it's irreparably injured, before it has no heartbeat and can't ever pang again.

Our life was in a good place in 2006. Bob had just been named co-anchor of *World News Tonight*, and although we knew that his job would require increasing amounts of travel, we also knew we would find a balance. Soon after he started his new gig, he went to report from Iraq for the eighth time in his career. This time, my husband was critically injured by a roadside bomb. That was a wake-up call—literally, at 7:00 a.m.—that no family should ever receive.

Even before the injury, I would have described us as a family who already "got it." We understood life was precious and short. Maybe we didn't live embracing that credo every single day, but who really does outside of an ashram? Anyway, we tried. We'd been through miscarriages, losing a child during pregnancy, a hysterectomy, the heartbreak of a child with a hearing disability, the tragic death of a close family friend. Together we had fingered the tenuous threads that hold us all here on earth, and these experiences had strengthened us as a couple in their aftermath.

A crisis often has a way of reprioritizing everything, and in an instant, my world was rocked. As I stared at him in his coma and listened to all the pronouncements of what the doctors thought he would and wouldn't be able to do when he emerged, I wanted more than anything else in the world for him to wake up, to talk to me, to make love one more time.

Over the next year I would become a devoted caregiver as our relationship went from equal footing to one that wobbled unevenly. All at once I was mother, nurse, and therapist. I was grieving the loss of someone who was still alive, but who had an uncertain future. With a head injury, no one can tell you how it will turn out, how much the patient will recover. What would this new man be like? What if, in the process of caring for him, I began to lose love? What if he remained broken and all of the things I respected—his intelligence, his ability to care for me— were in jeopardy?

I never thought for a minute about leaving. Not once. Maybe that's hard to believe, but I loved this man and I assumed that if he never returned to his former self, I would learn to love him in a different way. I even created a plan to ease my anxious mind during those regular 3:00 a.m. wake-ups: I would go back to work full time, sell the house, celebrate the things that were still there, the parts of my life that brought happiness. I would find ways, if I needed to, to fill the gaps in my soul with close girlfriends, stimulating conversation, and the escape of writing.

I had taken my wedding vows seriously and we'd enjoyed some amazing years together, full of extremes—we'd enjoyed both adventure and routine. We'd produced four terrific children. I would make our new situation work and honor him if he never really recovered. I would give him his dignity if he was unable to work again, no matter how tough that might be.

In the hospital, staring at his swollen head and his face mangled from the shrapnel, I decided that if he were going to be a vegetable, at least he would be my vegetable. I would take this day by day. There wasn't a doubt in my mind that he would do the same for me.

Luckily, my man returned. He came back in an amazing way, thanks to a lot of determination, time, and the love of family and friends. He has defied every expectation and his recovery is nothing short of a miracle. That's a pretty strong word, but I have to say it applies here. I'm not going to minimize or gloss over this process; it was hard work. I went through plenty of moments of despair and doubt and terror and grief. There was regret and sadness and depression, and on days when I had to buck everyone else up I felt emptier than a bottomless vessel. There are moments still where I can feel the damage that was done to all of us by that insurgent's bomb. Every trauma leaves its scars.

Once Bob was back at work and well on his way to becoming himself again, I crashed. The part of me that had been so "up" for all of those months as a necessity had to come down at some point. For months, I battled with the enormity of what had happened to us, the devastation and the post-traumatic stress giving way to disbelief and soul-sucking sorrow. And when I took that dive, Bob was there for me, just as I'd been for him. That's the amazing thing about a strong marriage: the give and take. Life is unpredictable, and sometimes all you can do is feel your way along with no road map. You use your gut and your toes, your instinct and your generosity, and you rely on one another. You may stumble sometimes, but if you've laid the groundwork and built the foundation, the center holds.

I don't recommend tragedy to bring people closer. I've known couples that divorced under the strain of illness or children with disease or disability. Hardship doesn't always bring out the best in people, and I can't pretend to have a formula for how it worked for us. I can say that not every day felt good or hopeful.

But as I write this in the bright sunlight of a July morning, four and a half years after his injury, my husband has already walked the dogs and gotten breakfast started. There is bacon on the stove and the trash is out by the curb. Our kids will be stirring soon and they will gradually tumble down the stairs in various states of awakening. At some point in the day, we will both look around us and be awash in the unarticulated goodness that makes up our lives. It's a feeling I have when I look at each member of my family and realize we have survived, and that our love has grown and aged in different ways; it is richer now, more mellow, like a good stinky cheese. We've mostly moved past that horrible time. The big thing that happened to us no longer defines us, and we are all moving forward.

Bob and I are closing in on a quarter century of marriage now. I can't tell you that we're religious about "date nights," having long, intricate conversations, or regular sex. Many times we don't even know what the other person is doing. I'm not always up on what news stories my husband is working on or where is he traveling on a given week, and he doesn't always know what articles I may be writing. Our lives are full and busy, and I am grateful for that—even though the side effects of being so busy can be stress, fatigue, and an occasional lost sense of connection.

Marriage is far more work than they ever tell you. Or maybe they do tell you and you just can't fathom it at the time. I think about that naïve couple we were, standing in front of the altar flanked by friends and family, believing that the whole world streamed out before us, that it was ours to fashion in a way of our choosing. And, to a degree, it was.

One of the hard things about surviving decades of marriage and life itself is to make peace with the fact that at a certain age, though you still feel mentally young, many of the roads have already been taken. The key choices have been made (unless you're a serial divorcée). There are no big surprises left—except possibly the ones you don't want to contemplate; the ones that involve loss. Don't get me wrong, there are still lots of wonderful moments to anticipate. But exciting, yet-to-be-revealed things like my choice of career, the man I'll marry, the children I'll raise—these blanks have all been filled in.

I often revisit a conversation I had a couple of years ago with a family friend, the mother of two boys my sisters and I grew up with during our summers in the Adirondack Mountains. At seventy-two she was dying of ovarian cancer, and she was honest and open about this fact when I went to visit her for what would be the last time. In that candid way you can afford to be with someone facing their own mortality, I asked her what advice she would give me about marriage; standing as I was, hopefully, in the middle of a long run.

"If I could do it over," she said, "I'd leave more dishes in the sink. I'd worry less about the to-do lists and leaving my kitchen perfect for the next day. I would have spent more time just sitting on my husband's lap."

What a heartbreakingly simple thing to do. Just sit there for a spell, entwined in one another. There is something so basic and pleasurable about it. You don't even need words. I try to remind myself of this advice as I rush through my day, fume over Bob's pile of dirty clothes on the floor, or slap together a microwaved family dinner. You'd think that after all I almost lost in my marriage, after everything we've been through as a family, I'd spend less time every day sweating the small stuff. But we have short memories. Real life intrudes and I have to remind myself of my friend's rearview mirror wisdom whenever I feel my foot pressing down on the accelerator.

There are hopefully many chapters yet unwritten in my marriage. But if you're just looking for the high-wire act, the roller-coaster thrill, if you're a junkie for the eternal sizzle, the fresh piece of flesh and the multiple orgasms, then my words are probably going to fall a little flat. Me? I'm simply happy that my husband and I can still reconnect to those parts of ourselves and one another that matter most, the things that brought us both together in the first place. I'm content most nights to aim for sitting on his lap.

Even if I don't get there as often as I should, I'm happy to focus on that next pang.

Note to self:

**There is no stronger glue
than laughter.**

ACKNOWLEDGMENTS

Rarely does a creative endeavor see the light of day without a forest full of fairies that believe in it and you and kindly sprinkle their magical dust to illuminate the idea and help bring it forth.

I've been blessed with a very rich and bountiful forest, and this book would not exist without the fearless and extremely talented contributors who so generously gave up their time so they could write about Love. And to those contributors who cried with me on the phone, who made me laugh so hard I snorted, who were afraid to write "the story" that had never been shared before, who are still grieving at the loss of their beloveds, or still in shock that their hearts are broken, or still madly in love with their husbands even after all these years, or blissfully alone and loving it, I thank each and every one of you from the bottom of my heart.

I have so much gratitude for the beautiful and kind Andrea Barzvi, who loves a good love story and who has been this book's biggest champion. And for Jennifer Bergstrom, whose heart is as big as her laugh, and whose support means the world to me.

Gratitude and beyond to my incredible team of editors: Emily Westlake, who, for the second time around, made each story sing with her meticulous mind, loving heart, and talented eye. NOLA is lucky to have you. Kara Cesare, the Italian Goddess, your name alone is comforting to the soul; working with you has been pure bliss. And Jennifer Smith, you literally kept the ball rolling with your lightning speed; it was such a treat working with you.

A big hearty thank you to the folks at S&S Gallery: Kristin Dwyer, who never says no; Jennifer Robinson; Michael Nagin; and Emilia Pisani.

And to those folks who took the time to say, "Hey, I know someone who would be great for your book," and then took even more time to put us in touch. My generous friends (old and new) Resa Wing, Maile Zambuto, Jordana Fraiberg, Mariska Hargitay, Katie Ford, Whitney Roberts, Beverly London, Brooke McMurray, Jayme Lemons, Katie Hnida, and John Nelson. A Huge Thank You!

Forever thank yous to all my friends and family who have lifted me up and kept me going every day in every way. And to the men and women of Tipi Tribe, I love you. And to Sherry Sidoti for introducing me to "The Layers."

And to my parents, Buck and Sue, who have been married since 1951 and are still in love. I know it hasn't always been easy, or perfect, but just knowing the two of you *together* has always been my biggest inspiration and the source of love for our entire family. I love you both, forever.

And last but not least, my husband, Jason Berkin; you have been my biggest and most profound teacher on the subject of love and an unwavering, undying, card-carrying supporter of us. I can't imagine life without you. So I won't even try. I love you and I am grateful for your love in return.